Naomi Wallace

the inland sea

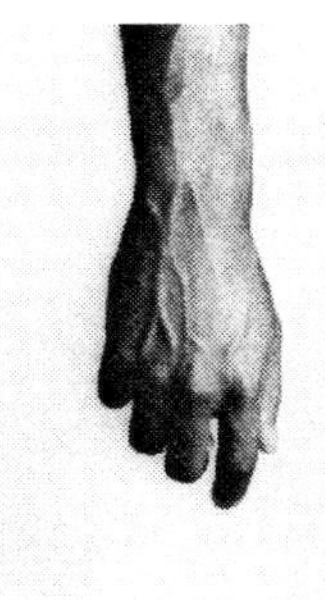

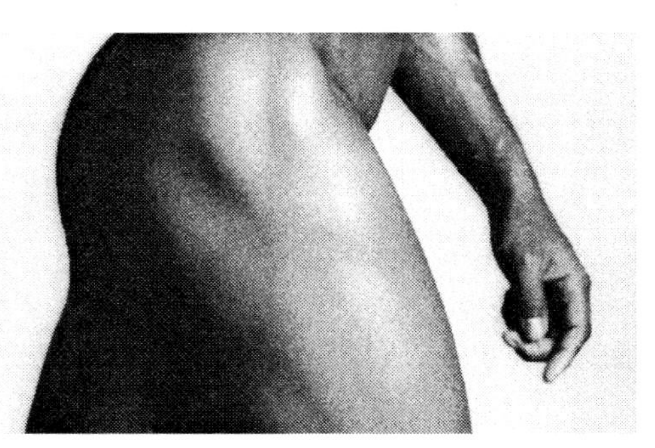

First performance of this production Wilton's Music Hall, London 3 April 2002

Oxford Stage Company is supported by

OXFORD STAGE COMPANY

Artistic Director
Dominic Dromgoole

Executive Producer
Conrad Lynch

Development Producer
Julia Hallawell

Associate Director
Sean Holmes

Administrator
Sandra Grieve

Finance Manager
Kris Sreekandath

'Oxford Stage Company has been one of the great success stories of recent years'
Daily Telegraph

Oxford Stage Company is committed to bringing together the highest calibre of actors, writers, directors and designers to create inspiring theatre that touches lives. Our aim is to expand the recognised canon of great plays - sometimes rediscovering neglected plays or writers, breathing fresh life into established classics or presenting adventurous new work, but always ensuring excellent, extraordinary theatre of merit which appeals to different people everywhere.

Our goal is to develop a consistently exciting education and access programme to accompany our tours and to continue giving the best young directors, designers and actors an opportunity to work on a challenging larger scale.

Oxford Stage Company
131 High Street
Oxford OX1 4DH
T 01865 723238
F 01865 790625
E info@oxfordstage.co.uk

the inland sea
by **Naomi Wallace**

Cast in order of appearance

ASH PIDDUCK, 'LEAFEATER'	**Peter Bourke**
LANCELOT 'CAPABILITY' BROWN	**Alan Williams**
ASQUITH BROWN	**Michael Gould**
HESP TURNER	**Jo McInnes**
SIMONE FAULKS	**Kate Duchêne**
BLISS	**Holly Scourfield**
JAYFORT	**Rhashan Stone**
CASTLE	**Jay Simpson**
SLIP	**James Lance**
SCARTH	**Michael Wilson**
NUTLEY	**William Mannering**
ELLEN	**Tricia Kelly**
VILLAGER 1	**Alan Williams**
VILLAGER 2	**Celia Delaney**
VILLAGER 3/ASM	**Jaison Beeson**
VILLAGER 4/ASM	**Jonathan Dryden Taylor**
VILLAGER 5	**Matthew Rutherford**

Writer **Naomi Wallace**

Director **Dominic Dromgoole**

Designer
Robert Innes Hopkins

Lighting Designer
Paul Anderson

Composer
Robert Lockhart

Sound Designer
Simon Whitehorn for Orbital Sound

Movement Director
Charlotte Conquest

Costume Supervisor
Sonaia Hermida

Dramaturg
Art Borreca

Assistant Dramaturg
Nancy Mayfield

Production Photography
John Haynes

London Press
Martin Shippen

Project Manager
Charlotte Bond

Production Manager
Jo Peake

Company Manager
Lindah Balfour

Deputy Stage Manager
Julia Reid

Assistant Stage Manager
Jesse Kate Kramer

Box Office Co-ordinator
Helen Hillman

Education Co-ordinator
Jacqui Somerville

BIOGRAPHIES

Jaison Beeson Villager 3/ASM

Training: Guildhall School of Music and Drama

Theatre: Forty Years On (Palace Theatre Westcliff); *The Sound of Fury* (UK tour); *Ferry Cross the Mersey* (West End and tour); *Walking on Sunshine* (UK tour) and *The Roy Orbison Story* (UK tour).

Television: *Peak Practice, The Bill, Agony* and various commercials.

Film: *The Changeling* and *Wolf in an Aran Sweater*.

Other: Corporate videos for Abbey National and West Yorkshire Police.

Peter Bourke Ash Pidduck, 'Leafeater'

Training: RADA

Theatre: For the Royal Shakespeare Company: *Henry IV* Parts 1 and 2, *Henry V* and *Perkin Warbeck*. For the Royal National Theatre: *The Browning Version, Harlequinade, The Elephant Man, The Provoked Wife* and *On the Razzle*. West End credits include: *When We Are Married, Exclusive, Dial M For Murder* and *Endgame*. Seasons at Chichester include: *The Merry Wives of Windsor, Racing Demon, The Sea* and *A Christmas Carol*. On tour: *Bedroom Farce, Donkeys Years, One Flew Over the Cuckoo's Nest*. Other theatre includes *Single Spies, Volpone* (Salisbury Playhouse), *Woman in Mind, Picture of Dorian Gray* and *Gingerbread Lady* (Palace Theatre Watford).

Television: *Nicholas Nickleby, David Copperfield, Mayor of Casterbridge, Traffic* and *Hazel*. TV plays include *Reluctant Chickens, Iniciation* and *America America*.

Film: *Stand Up Virgin Soldiers, The Stud, The Mission* and *SOS Titanic*.

Other: For Fair Play Theatre Company, Peter has Actor Managed the West End premiere of *Endgame* and the world premieres of *Sketches by Boz* (Battersea Arts Centre and tour) and *The Suitcase Kid* (Tricycle Theatre and Brix).

Celia Delaney Villager 2

Training: Mountview Theatre School

Theatre: Credits include Cathy in *Wuthering Heights* (Wimbledon Theatre and national tour); Rosaline in *Love's Labours' Lost* (C Theatre Company); Kate in *She Stoops to Conquer* (The Royal George); Jacqueline in *French Without Tears* (Maddermarket, Norwich) and the title role in *Catherine Booth* (national tour).

Television: *Waiting Women* (Channel 4) and *Dinodiet* (Discovery Channel)

Jonathan Dryden Taylor Villager 4

Training: National Youth Music Theatre

Theatre: *Storeys* (Steam Industry); *Troilus and Cressida* (Old Vic); *50 Revolutions* and *A Penny for a Song* (OSC/Whitehall Theatre); *King Lear, Twelfth Night* (national tour); *Inkle and Yarico, Eurydice* (Straydogs at Battersea Arts Centre); *October's Children* (Swan, Stratford and Sadler's Wells). As a director, *The Liar* (Edinburgh Festival), *Odes and Gameshows* (CPT) and *Macbeth and the Beanstalk* (Pleasance London).

Television: *Oedipus the King* and *Two Gentleman of Verona* (BBC).

Film: *One Colour, White*.

Other: Numerous plays and serials for BBC Radio. Adaptation and translation work includes *The Liar* (Edinburgh), Boccacio's *Decameron* (BBC Radio 4) and *Trumpets and Raspberries* (The Gate).

Kate Duchêne Simone Faulks

Theatre: Credits include *Arturo Ui* and *The Miser* (Royal National Theatre); *Richard III, The Country Wife, The Cherry Orchard* and *The Herbal Bed* (Royal Shakespeare Company); *Hated Nightfall* (The Wrestling School) and *Iphigenia in Aulis* (Abbey Theatre Dublin).

Television: *Midsomer Murders, Kiss Me Kate, The Worst Witch, Peak Practice* and *Out of Hours*.

Film: *The Tall Guy*.

Michael Gould Asquith Brown

Training: Academy of Live and Recorded Arts

Theatre: Credits include Edmund in *King Lear*, Polixenes in *The Winter's Tale* and Diphilus in *A Maid's Tragedy* (Shakespeare's Globe Theatre); Hatch in *The Sea* and John Knill in *The King of Prussia* (Chichester Festival Theatre); Agamemnon/Apollo in *The Oresteia* (Royal National Theatre); Benvolio in *Romeo and Juliet*, Creon in *The Phoenician Women*, Rosencrantz in *Hamlet* (Royal Shakespeare Company); Richard in *Dead Funny* and Huntingdon in *The Tenant of Wildfell Hall* (New Victoria Theatre); Angelo in *Measure for Measure* and Malvolio in *Twelfth Night* (A & BC Theatre); Debray in *The Count of Monte Cristo* (Manchester Royal Exchange) and Rousard in *The Atheists Tragedy* (Birmingham Rep).

Television: *EastEnders, The Bill, Bliss, The World of Lee Evans* and *History File*.

Film: Mary Shelley's *Frankenstein*.

Radio: *The Care Takers* and *Aria for Alf*.

Tricia Kelly Ellen

Theatre: *Some Explicit Polaroids* (Out of Joint UK and international tour); *Local* (Royal Court Upstairs); *Julius Caesar* and *Ion* (RSC); *Juno and the Paycock* (National Theatre); *Victory, Seven Lears, Golgo, The Last Supper* and Ego In Arcadia (The Wrestling School); *Fen, Deadlines* and *A Mouthful of Birds* (Joint Stock/Royal Court); *Sunsets & Glories, Two, Not I* and *King Lear* (West Yorkshire Playhouse); *Seasons Greetings, Julius Caesar* and *The Whisper of Angels' Wings* (Birmingham Repertory Theatre); *The Government Inspector, The Seagull* and *As You Like It* (The Crucible, Sheffield); *A Wife Without A Smile, The Cassilis Engagement, The House Among The Stars, Court In The Act* and *The Last Thrash* (Orange Tree, Richmond); *Amphytryon* (The Gate); East Lynne (Greenwich Theatre); *Dancing at Lughnasa* (Salisbury Playhouse); *Top Girls* (Lancaster); *The Voysey Inheritance* (UK tour – Royal Lyceum Theatre & Edinburgh International Theatre Festival).

TV: *Casualty, My Family, High Stakes, B&B, In Sickness and In Health, This is David Landor, Dangerous Lady* and an *Omnibus* on Caryl Churchill.

Film: *Top Dog, Big Feet* and *A Small Dance*.

James Lance Slip

Theatre: *A Penny for a Song* (OSC/Whitehall Theatre); *A Place at the Table* and *The Back Room* (Bush Theatre); *Brilliant the Dinosaur* (Royal Festival Hall) and *Elegies for Angels, Punks and Raging Queens* (Criterion Theatre)

Television: *I'm Alan Patridge* (BBC), *Rescue Me* (BBC), *Teachers* (Channel 4), *The Book Group* (Channel 4), *Smack the Pony* (Channel 4), *Spaced* (Channel 4), *People Like Us* (BBC), *Absolutely Fabulous* (BBC) and *Family Money* (Channel 4).

Film: *Late Night Shopping, The Search for John Gissing, Subterrain* and *Fistful of Fingers*.

William Mannering Nutley

Theatre: *The Winter's Tale* and *The Lion, The Witch and The Wardrobe* (RSC); *Vincent River* (Hampstead Theatre); *The Winslow Boy* (The Globe); *Divine Right* and *The Merchant of Venice* (Birmingham Repertory Theatre) and *The Golden Crown* (Leatherhead).

TV: *Dalziel and Pascoe, Beck, Casualty, The Bill, Urban Gothic,*

Unfinished Business, Wuthering Heights, Black Hearts in Battersea, Coral Island, Heartbeat, The Infinite Worlds of HG Wells, Cadfael, Sharpe, Medics, The Upper Hand and *Space Vets*.

Film: *Breaking the Code, Jackpot* and *The Old Curiosity Shop*.

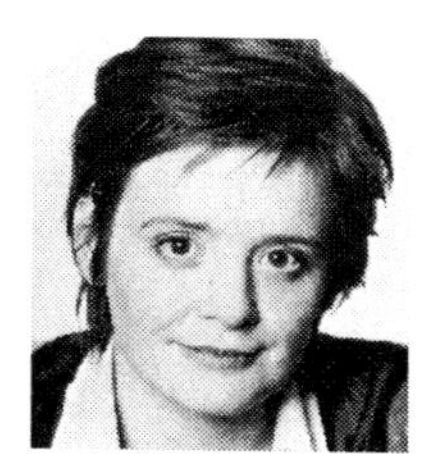

Jo McInnes Hesp

Theatre: Credits include *Edward II* (Crucible Theatre, Sheffield); *4.48 Psychosis and Bluebird* (Royal Court); *Playhouse Creatures* (Old Vic); *The Children's Hour* (National Theatre); *Uncle Vanya, The Herbal Bed* and *The General From America* (RSC); *Biloxi Blues, The Importance of Being Earnest, Private Lives, Memoirs of a Survivor* and *Billy Liar* (Salisbury Playhouse); *The Last of the Just* (Arts Theatre); *Romeo and Juliet* (Angels Theatre) and *The Mayflies* (Attic Theatre).

TV: *Playing The Field, Soldier, Soldier* and *Casualty*.

Film: *My Wife's An Actress, Birthday Girl, Gangster No 1 and The New Romantics*.

Other: Radio includes *Scars and Uncertainty* for Radio 4. Jo received an Ian Charleston commendation in 1998.

Matthew Rutherford Villager 5

Training: BA. Ed (Hons) in Theatre Studies from University College Chester

Theatre: Matthew spent two seasons touring Europe with Riding Lights Theatre Company, where his credits include *Bet Your Life, A Different Drum, On Christmas Night* and *Roughshod Gospel*. His two years with the Yorkshire-based theatre company were punctuated with various roles in the Chester *Mystery Plays* of 1997. Playing the part of Joe B. Mauldin in the West End production of *The Buddy Holly Story*, Matthew delighted in some work stability and grabbed the opportunity to marry the lovely Sadie.

Television: *The Devil: An Unauthorised Biography* (BBC1) and *Peter's Story* (Tandem TV).

Film: *Jules on a Train*.

Holly Scourfield Bliss

Training: Holly has trained at Stage 84 Stage School in Bradford since the age of three.

Theatre: *My Fair Lady, Fiddler on the Roof* and *Guys and Dolls* all at the Edinburgh Fringe Festival.

Television: Holly has appeared in *The Bill*, *Fat Friends*, written by Kay Mellor, *Children's Ward*, *Where the Heart Is* and is due to appear in a second series of *Fat Friends* which has just finished filming and an episode in the series *Wire in the Blood*.

Film: Holly had the lead role in a TV film entitled *When I Was Twelve*, for which she has been nominated as Best Newcomer on Screen for the Royal Television Society Awards.

Jay Simpson Castle

Theatre: *Mother Clapp's Molly House* (Royal National Theatre and Aldwych Theatre); *Battle Royal* (Royal National Theatre); *The Good Samaritan* and *No Experience Required* (Hampstead Theatre); *Richard III* (Pleasance Theatre); *Afters*, *Hummingbird* and *Golden Own Goal* (Old Red Lion) and *Srebrenica* (Tricycle Theatre)

Television: *The Firm*, *Hot Money*, *Casualty*, *The Bill*, *A Touch of Frost*, *Thieftakers*, *The Thin Blue Line* and *London's Burning*. Jay will appear in a new series called *Falling Down* in May.

Film: *Erik the Viking*, *Beautiful People*, *Club Le Monde*, *This Year's Love* and *SW4*.

Rhashan Stone Jayfort

Theatre: Credits include *Sing Your Heart Out for the Lads* (Royal National Theatre); *Clubland* (Royal Court Theatre); *This England*. The Histories: *Henry VI* (Parts I, II & III), *Richard III*, *Hamlet*, *Much Ado About Nothing* and *Camino Real* (Royal Shakespeare Company); *The Tempest*, *Present Laughter* and *The Seagull* (West Yorkshire Playhouse); *Sweeney Todd* and *The Red Balloon* (Royal National Theatre); *A Funny Thing Happened on the Way to the Forum* and *The Merry Wives of Windsor* (New Shakespeare Company); *As You Like It* (Cheek by Jowl world tour and West End); *Animal Crackers* (Manchester Royal Exchange), *Happy End* and *Doughnuts* (Nottingham Playhouse); *Generations of the Dead* (Contact Theatre); *Chasing the Moment* (RNT Studio, Pleasance Theatre and Battersea Arts Centre) and *Five Guys Named Moe* (Lyric Theatre).

Television: Credits include *Fifteen Storeys High*, *Holby City*, *Picking Up the Pieces*, *The Detectives*, *Goodnight Sweetheart* and *Desmonds*.

Alan Williams
Lancelot 'Capability' Brown/Villager 1

Training: Manchester Youth Theatre.

Theatre: *The Darling Family* (Theatre Passe Muraille, Toronto); *Vigil* (Vancouver Arts Club); *Crave* (Paines Plough - Traverse/Royal Court); *The Jew of Malta* (Almeida); *Local* (Royal Court).

TV: *Always and Everyone*, *Sirens* and *The Wire in the Blood*.

Film: *The Cockroach that Ate Cincinnati*, *Among Giants*, *The Darling Family* and *Heartlands*.

Michael Wilson Scarth

Training: Webber Douglas Academy of Dramatic Art

Theatre: *Bread and Butter* (Southwark Playhouse); *Knives in Hens* (Tour); *There Are Crimes and Crimes* and *A View From The Bridge* (Leicester Haymarket); *Loot* (Leatherhead); *Of Mice and Men* (Harrogate Theatre); *Half Moon* (Battersea Arts Centre and tour); *The School of Night* (Chichester Festival Theatre); *The Mousetrap* (Tour); *Macbeth* (Arts Theatre); *The Suitcase Kid* (Tricycle Theatre); *Boot* (Man in the Moon Theatre); *Boudicca's Victory* (Riverside Studios).

TV: *Close Relations*, *The Knock*, *Hale & Pace*, *EastEnders*, *The Bill*, *Side by Side* and *Trainer*.

Film: *The Titchbourne Claimant*, *Anxiety* and *When Only Love Still Counts*.

CREATIVE TEAM

Naomi Wallace Writer

Naomi's last stage play *The Trestle at Pope Lick Creek* received its UK premiere at the Traverse Theatre, Edinburgh in February 2001. It was the highlight of the 1998 Humana Festival at Louisville and opened at New York Theatre Workshop in June 1999. In 1999 Naomi was awarded the MacArthur Fellowship.

Naomi's first feature film *Lawn Dogs* opened in the UK at the London Film Festival in November 1997, having won the Best Screenplay award at the Sitges Film Festival. It was produced by Duncan Kenworthy (*Four Weddings And A Funeral*) and directed by John Duigan.

Naomi's London West End debut was in 1997 with her stage adaptation of William Wharton's classic novel *Birdy*, which opened in February, following highly successful runs at London's Lyric Theatre, Hammersmith and the Drum Theatre, Plymouth in 1996. Naomi's New York debut took place four days later at the Joseph Papp Public Theatre in March 1997 with *One Flea Spare*, winning the prestigious Obie Award for Best New Play. The play was first produced in 1995 at the Bush Theatre, London which also produced *In the Heart of America*.

Naomi's Mobil Playwriting Competition prize-winning play *Slaughter City* received its world premiere at the RSC in January 1996 and its US premiere shortly afterwards with The American Repertory Theatre. Her first production for the stage was *The War Boys* at London's Finborough Theatre in 1993. Naomi also co-wrote *In The Sweat* with Bruce McLeod for the National Theatre's Education Department for the 1997 BT/National Connections.

Naomi's poetry has been published on both sides of the Atlantic. She has won the National Poetry Prize in America and in 1995 her first poetry collection, *To Dance A Stony Field*, was published in the UK by Peterloo Poets.

Dominic Dromgoole Director

Dominic Dromgoole was appointed Artistic Director of Oxford Stage Company in September 1998. For OSC he has produced *Making Noise Quietly, Three Sisters, 50 Revolutions, A Penny for a Song, Troilus and Cressida, The Circle, The Wexford Trilogy, The Contractor, Hay Fever, Top Girls* and *Comedians*.

In 1997 Dominic was New Plays Director of the Old Vic alongside Sir Peter Hall where he produced six new plays, directing two. From 1990-96 Dominic ran the Bush Theatre in west London where, as a producer, he put together sixty-five world or British premieres. Two Bush productions transferred to the West End, *Beautiful Thing* and *Killer Joe*. Dominic directed nine plays at the Bush. He has also directed in Louisville, Kentucky for the Humana Festival, in Florence for the Intercity Festival, and in Romania.

Dominic's first book, *The Full Room*, an overview of contemporary playwriting, has recently been published by Methuen. He is also Associate Producer of the film *Saltwater*.

Robert Innes Hopkins Designer

Robert trained at Nottingham Polytechnic and was a finalist in the 1991 Linbury Prize. In 1996, Robert won the Critics' Circle Designer of the Year Award for *The Comedy of Errors* (RSC) and *The Weavers* (The Gate). In 1997, he won the TMA Designer of the Year Award for *The Wasp Factory* (West Yorkshire Playhouse) and *My Mother Said I Never Should* (Oxford Stage Company).

Other theatre includes *The Villains' Opera* (Royal National Theatre) and *A Servant to Two Masters* (RSC). Opera includes *The Bartered Bride* (for which he received a nomination in the 1999 TMA Awards - Outstanding Achievement in Opera) and *The Elixir of Love* (Opera North). Recent work includes *Redundant*

(Royal Court Theatre Downstairs); *Paradise Moscow* (Opera North); *I Capuletie I Montecchi* (Grange Park Opera); and Wozzeck (Santa Fe Opera). Future work includes *Rigoletto* (Welsh National Opera).

Paul Anderson Lighting Designer

Paul trained at Mountview Theatre School and York College of Arts and Technology. Productions include *The Noise of Time*, *Light*, *Mnemonic* (for which he received the 2001 Drama Desk & Lucille Lortel Awards) and *The Chairs* (Tony, Drama Desk & Olivier Award nominations) (Theatre de Complicite); *Arabian Nights*, *As I Lay Dying*, *Twelfth Night*, *West Side Story* and *Guys & Dolls* (Young Vic); *A Servant to Two Masters* (RSC), *Pinnochio* and *The Threesome* (Lyric Theatre, Hammersmith); *Shoot to Win*, *Aladdin* and *Cinderella* (Theatre Royal, Stratford East). Other recent designs include *Twelfth Night* (Shakespeare's Globe at Middle Temple Hall), *Lyric Nights* (World Music at Lyric Theatre, Hammersmith) *Colour in Design* (Lancôme) and *The Christie Brown Exhibition* (Wapping Pumping Station). He is currently designing *The Birds* for the Royal National Theatre. Paul is also the Managing Director of Sparks Theatrical Hire Limited the lighting hire specialist.

Robert Lockhart Composer

Training: Oxford University (double first honours degree in music); Royal College of Music (piano and composition).

Theatre: *One Flea Spare* (The Bush); *Threepenny Opera* and *The Pied Piper* (National Theatre - Musical Director 1986-9); *The Merchant of Venice* and *Map of the Heart* (West End); *Jekyll and Hyde* (RSC at the Barbican); *Preserving Mr Panmure*, *The Silver King* and *On the Razzle* (Chichester Theatre).

TV: *Inspector Lynley Mysteries*, *The Safe House*, *Between The Lines* (which received a BAFTA nomination), *Grafters*, *Unnatural Pursuits* and *The Bullion Boys*.

Film: *Cold Comfort Farm*, *Distant Voices*, *Still Lives*, *The Long Day Closes*, *The Neon Bible*, *On the Black Hill* and *Vicious Circles*.

Robert has also given regular recitals as a pianist at the Wigmore Hall, Fairfield Hall, the Purcell Room, the Aldeburgh Festival and on BBC Radio 3.

Simon Whitehorn for Orbital Sound Sound Designer

Previous West End productions include *The Constant Wife* (Apollo); *Cat on a Hot Tin Roof* (Lyric); *Entertaining Mr Sloane* (Arts); *Playboy of the Western World*, *Singin' in the Rain*, *The Riot* and *The Villains Opera* (Royal National Theatre); *The Seven Year Itch* and *Hurlyburly* (Queen's); *Cooking With Elvis*, *Three Sisters* and *The Slow Drag* (Whitehall); *The Birthday Party* (Piccadilly), *Forbidden Broadway* (Albery); *Salad Days* and *Killer Joe* (Vaudeville); *Birdy* (Comedy); *Prayers of Sherkin*, *Gracenote*, *Playhouse Creatures*, *Snake in the Grass* and *Shining Souls* (Peter Hall season at Old Vic).

During fourteen seasons at the Open Air Theatre, Regent's Park, he has designed many Shakespeare plays and the musicals *Pirates of Penzance*, *Where's Charley?*, *A Funny Thing Happened on the Way to the Forum*, *Gentlemen Prefer Blondes*, *Kiss Me Kate*, *Paint Your Wagon* and *The Fantasticks*. Other work includes *Comedians* (OSC); *The Kingfisher* (tour); *The Best of Times* (Bridewell); *Singin' in the Rain* and *The Pirates of Penzance* (West Yorkshire Playhouse); *Stop Kiss*, *Be My Baby*, *Angels and Saints*, *Noise and Skeleton* (Soho Theatre); *Flesh and Blood* and *Jude the Obscure* (Method and Madness); *All's Well That Ends Well* (Manchester Royal Exchange); *Normal*, *The Backroom*, *Dogs Barking*, *Card Boys* and *Love You Too* (Bush Theatre). Simon is a member of the design department at Orbital Sound.

Charlotte Conquest Movement Director

Charlotte trained at Middlesex University. Work as a movement director/choreographer includes: *Augustine's Oak* (Shakespeare's Globe); *As You Like It, Midsummer Night's Dream, The Man Who Would Be King, Cinderella* and Northanger Abbey (Northcott Theatre, Exeter); *Shelf Life* (Southwark Playhouse); *A Little Night Music* (Arts Educational); *Orfeo* (Kent Opera); *Don Giovanni* (Royal Academy of Music); *Grease* (Bellaby Theatre, Guildford) and *George Dandin* (Red Shift). Work as a director includes for theatre: *Bedroom Farce, A Curlew's Cry, The Turn of the Screw, The Grapes of Wrath* (co-director), *Northanger Abbey* (co-director) and *Single Spies* (Northcott Theatre); *Chasing Dolphins* (Churchill, Bromley); *2000 Fine Lines* (Machine Room); *Underbelly* (London New Play Festival); *Between Love and Passion* (New End); *Blood Wedding, Roberto Zucco* (Arts Educational); *As You Like It* (Creation Theatre Company) and *The Window Ranter* (RSC staged reading). For TV: *Doctors* (3 episodes for BBC) *Funny Thing Life* (Television Arts Performance Showcase). Work as assistant director: *Othello* (RSC); *The London Cuckolds* (RNT) and *Death in Venice* (Red Shift). Charlotte is currently resident director on Trevor Nunn's · National Theatre production of South Pacific. Later this year Charlotte is working on more episodes of *Doctors* for the BBC.

Sonaia Hermida Costume Supervisor

Sonaia has been working as a Costume Designer for television, theatre and advertising since 1987. She left Brazil 11 years ago to study Costume Design and after her studies, she worked for the Shakespeare Globe Museum. Her latest work includes Noel Coward's 1930s *Red Peppers* and *Still Life*; *This Is Our Youth*, by Kenneth Lonergan, now showing at the Garrick Theatre.

HISTORICAL NOTES

A Century of Change

The Inland Sea is set in the 1760s, at a time of major social and economic change. The first half of the century, before the time of the play, had seen a wave of population growth. It had also seen an agricultural revolution, with new tools (the mechanical drill and hoe) and more productive methods of planting and harvesting. The 1760s came at the height of that revolution, as well as at the start of the shift from a largely agricultural to an emerging industrial society.

With these changes, the class-structure was also changing. From the start of the century, 'the middling classes' had expanded, coming to include tenant farmers and yeomen, merchants and tradespeople, skilled labourers (such as shipbuilders), among others. That expansion, however, hinged on the increasing wealth of the aristocracy and gentry and the rising poverty of the poorest members of society.

At the top of society, fortunes were growing with steep rises in foreign and transatlantic trade, especially in the slave trade. Over the course of the century, British slave traders transported 1 1/2 million Africans to the West Indies alone.

At the bottom of society, a new kind of poverty developed, resulting not from war or famine but from under-nourishment. Although productivity had risen, so had farm profits and food prices. In relation to the population as a whole, food had become scarce. In the 1760s, machine-breaking and 'strike sails' for higher wages were commonplace in London. In the countryside, landowners had incomes ranging from £8,000 to £30,000 per year, while farm labourers got by on an average of 5 to 7 shillings per week.

The Changing Landscape

The social and economic changes of the period were being written visibly into the land. At the start of the century, about half of all arable land had been cultivated on the 'open field' system of farming, with common fields broken into strips held by various families. As the century progressed, patterns of enclosed fields, marked by walls, fences, hedgerows, and roads, spread throughout the countryside.

The process of enclosing lands had begun before 1750 but accelerated in the 1760s. Ultimately, Parliament legitimized the process with a long series of Enclosure Acts favouring the landowners and denying legal rights to copyholders and squatters.

Whereas at the start of the century the peerage of England had owned 15-20% of the land, by the end it would own 20-25%. All landowners, gentry as well as aristocracy, would own three-quarters of all cultivated land, most of it leased to tenant farmers.

Around the time of the play, new laws regulating the use of land and wild game were being established. These were enforced by local magistrates and Justices of the Peace drawn mostly from the landed gentry. New philosophical-legal concepts of 'absolute ownership' and 'private property' were being written into the legal system.

The laws gave birth to an army of wardens and gamekeepers, whose job it was to carry out the less pleasant aspects of landowning. Gamekeepers watched over the wild game on an estate, preserving it to be hunted by the owner and his peers. The laws against poaching were severe, but the gamekeepers often took justice into their own hands.

Redesigning Nature

The wealthiest and most powerful landowners went beyond enclosing to 'imparking' their estates – transforming the grounds of their estates into landscaped parks, and often tearing down buildings, pre-existing gardens, and forests. They even razed, relocated, or drowned villages that obstructed the view.

Viscount Cobham razed the village of Stowe, removing its inhabitants to Dadford. Thomas Coke moved the village of Holkham but later expressed some remorse: 'It is a melancholy thing to stand alone in one's own country. I look around, not a house to be seen but for my own. I am Giant, of Giant's Castle, and have ate up all my neighbours.'

The most famous English landscape designer, Lancelot Brown (1715-1783) was nicknamed 'Capability' due to his fondness for saying that a country estate had great 'capability' for improvement. Eventually given the position of Master Gardener to King George III, Brown's landscapes eradicated architectural gardens of French and Italian classical design, replacing them with sweeping expanses of lawn, undulating hills, and picturesque groupings of trees.

Brown was also responsible for the introduction of new species of trees to the English landscape, especially North American conifers. Along with his designs, his use of such trees changed the face of the English countryside.

Brown's landscapes spread a new idea of artfully cultivated 'nature.' For the lords, landscaping was part of the cultivation and display of aesthetic taste and sensibility. It went hand in hand with the collections of artwork, antiques, and books to which they dedicated entire rooms of their mansions. Beneath the aesthetics of a Capability Brown landscape, however, there was the political will to keep the rising numbers of the impoverished out of view.

The Inland Sea: Fact and Fiction

The year in which *The Inland Sea* is set, 1763, came at the end of the Seven Years War. The play is based on Capability Brown and the eighteenth-century landscape movement, which was at its height at the time. However, the play is fiction.

Capability Brown was the fifth of sixth children. Although he had a younger brother about whom little is known, his brother in the play, Asquith, is a fictitional character.

The Lord of the estate in the play, Lord Heywood is also a fiction. However, Capability Brown designed more than fifty estates, including Blenheim, Stowe, Sherborne, and an estate for a Lord Harewood in Yorkshire. The play refers to Compton Verney, Syon House, Alnwick, Radley, and Burghly, all of which were completed in the approximate time period of the play.

In the play, Brown refers to William Chambers' *A Dissertation on Oriental Gardening*. The book was not in fact published until 1772, after the time of the play.

A note on the character of Jayfort. In the eighteenth century, London became a centre for organized boxing or prize fighting, which was a favourite spectator sport among the upper-classes. Most boxers came from the working class and boxing was one of the few means by which blacks could rise in status. Many blacks also became merchant seaman, an occupation of lower status, but one in which blacks were widely accepted.

Notes compiled by Art Borreca with the assistance of Nancy Mayfield.

Naomi Wallace
The Inland Sea

faber and faber

First published in 2002
by Faber and Faber Limited
3 Queen Square, London WC1N 3AU

Typeset by Country Setting, Kingsdown, Kent CT14 8ES
Printed in England by Intype London Ltd

A CIP record for this book
is available from the British Library

ISBN 0-571-21668-4

2 4 6 8 10 9 7 5 3 1

The great force of history comes from the fact that we carry it within us, are unconsciously controlled by it in many ways, and history is literally present in all that we do.

James Baldwin

For this is where we live, we who are not martyrs.

Raymond Williams

Characters

Lancelot 'Capability' Brown
landscape designer, forty-nine years old

Asquith Brown
his brother, assistant landscape designer, thirty-eight years

Ash Pidduck
also known as 'Leafeater', late fifties

Hesp Turner
a woman villager, mid-thirties

Simone Faulks
a landscape artist, visitor of Lord Heywood, thirties

Bliss
a young girl, eleven.

Jayfort
sailor, Jamaican origins

Castle
shipbuilder, from London

Slip
shipbuilder, from London

Scarth
soldier hired out for digging

Nutley
soldier hired out for digging

Ellen
villager, Hesp's mother, mid-fifties

Four Villagers
(Villager One and Four are male)

Time
1760s

Place
The grounds of a large estate in Yorkshire.

Set
The set is minimal, clear, sweeping, astonishingly beautiful as a landscape, and not realistic.

Notes
There is no overlapping of dialogue.
Interruption is indicated. A full stop anywhere indicates a break or brief pause.

The quotation at the end of Act One is from Milton's *Paradise Lost*, Book XI, lines 691-699.

Prologue

In the dark we hear the sounds of the countryside, birds mostly, but the sounds are 'off' or slightly disembodied. Among these sounds the faint sound of a shovel, digging in the earth. This sound increases until it overwhelms the other sounds.

As first light appears, a figure is seen digging, or more likely covering a hole in the ground. Then we realise it is Leafeater. The burying is careful and unhurried, but the figure is wearied.

Leafeater leans down to pick up something and put it in his pocket. And yet the sound of the shovel continues for some moments. He slowly walks away from the mound, dragging the shovel behind, the blade of which makes an eerie sound as it drags.

But then Leafeater stops, pauses, then turns and walks back to the 'mound' and stands over it.

Leafeater Leave.

A moment of silence.

Me alone.

Blackout.

Act One

SCENE ONE

Guest cottage on Lord Heywood's estate. Lancelot 'Capability' Brown and his brother, Asquith, are studying the plans for the grounds. Lancelot has asthma, but only coughs where noted.

Lancelot Ah, Ah. Watch your finger there, you're smudging the *Pinus radiata*. Plant them along the north side. Excellent wind breakers. Along this ridge, the American pines. The saplings should arrive by the end of the week. Lord Heywood will be travelling. I've encouraged him to stay away during the early stages. He's attached to the old gardens, poor man. Now, the old hedges, there and here, almost three miles of them, and across here, out. Three formal gardens, put them under. Both large and small fountains, twelve in all, gone. And the river, here, we will bend her so that she will look like a substantial lake. Now, I want the lawn brought right up to the steps this time. We are going to island Lord Heywood's great house in a sea of lawn so that he will find dew on his slippers the moment he steps through the door . . .

Lancelot breaks into an asthmatic cough. Asquith waits for it to pass. When it does, Lancelot just stares suddenly at Asquith a few moments.

No whoring either, brother. This is a commission of some importance and cannot be undone by loose breeches.

Asquith No. Of course. Of course not. That happened only once, I never –

Lancelot (*interrupts*) A whore is like a foreign garden on English soil: perfumed, seductive, but ultimately nothing but a painted ruin. All style and no substance. Get a wife – it concentrates the mind. (*Lancelot goes to the plans again.*)

Asquith You're very kind to think of me –

Lancelot Ah, but I am not kind when I wash away the imported stink, on estate after estate, of these little claustrophobic theatres of excess, these gaudy display cabinets that too many call gardens. No. Kindness is to be reserved for your wife – when you get one, that is.

Asquith How are Bridget and the children?

Lancelot In good health, I thank God. They keep their spirits up despite my travelling.

Asquith You'll be in Burghly the next two months then?

Lancelot Yes. Seven miles of grounds there. A delicious bastard, that job. The waters I've combined make twenty-seven acres . . .

Lancelot puts his arm around Asquith's shoulders and turns him towards the vision he imagines.

And today, my brother, if you stand before the Earl of Exeter's house, it looks as though the lake were now a river rolling to meet you.

Asquith (*joining in this vision, creating a 'union'*) No obstructions, no horticultural excess –

Lancelot Not a fountain or terrace or balustrade left to be seen. A truly English garden born at Burghly. No frills, just wide open spaces . . .

Lancelot is done with this 'union' but Asquith presses on with his enthusiasm.

Asquith . . . and the new trees softening the hard edges in the distance, laid out in clusters, with no apparent mathematical design, no enforced geometry, creating a landscape that appears to have grown up entirely by chance . . .

Lancelot Exactly. Bah. Those formal gardens. As rigid as corpses they are, and as sweet in the sun. They're not for the living.

Asquith (*continuing*) That's right! Away with the fiddlesome French, the fastidious Italian designs. And all across the bright green oceanic lawns –

Lancelot (*uncertain*) Oceanic lawns . . .

Lancelot breaks the moment with a hard, short coughing fit and goes to roll up the plans. He is somewhat surprisingly harsh here, as though he were punishing his brother.

I wouldn't go quite that far. This is all mere grass and mud we're dealing with here.

Silence some moments.

Asquith (*quietly*) The village you intend to move. It is not sure it wants to move.

Lancelot What do you mean?

Asquith Some of the villagers want to stay.

Lancelot (*studies plan*) Well, it's not in my plan.

Asquith We'll build them a new village. I'll take care of the design. They're just uncertain. It's the change they fear.

Lancelot Of course. And Lord Heywood has always dealt fairly with his people. Not even poachers were hung in the black years. The villagers trust him. Don't damage that trust.

Silence some moments.

Asquith You were lucky with Bridget. As you rose, you took her with you. The ladies of the class we move in still flinch when I take their hand, afraid that the dirt of my childhood is still on my sleeves. Women below me, I cannot trust their intentions.

Lancelot (*trying to be light*) Still having those nightmares that you are trapped inside a lighthouse? And yourself, the one sole light calling out unanswered?

Asquith looks away, hurt but still haunted.

Asquith The waters are wild and black. And cold. They rise over me. I wake because I cannot. Breathe.

Lancelot Hmm. My suggestion is make sure your sleeves are always clean in the company of ladies. To act a born gentleman is more difficult than being one. So act well.

Returning to the plans.

Any other problems you foresee?

Asquith Not at this time –

Lancelot (*hardly listening*) Asquith. You are not merely my representative here. Unlike the other projects, this one I give completely into your hands.

Asquith And you know that I –

Lancelot (*interrupts*) And it is conceivable that if this plan goes well, perhaps you might design the next one yourself. Such is the trust I have in you.

Asquith I am truly grateful.

Lancelot Remember, my brother, whatever you create out there, as far as the eye can see, is the story of who you are – (*Lancelot thumps Asquith's chest gently.*) – in here.

SCENE TWO

Some weeks later. It is a bright day, early morning, in Yorkshire, 1763. The sounds of nature are heard clearly. It is early spring but still cold. Three men, Jayfort, Slip and Castle, are digging out a trench.

Castle For one simple reason: when they fly, they shit on your head.

Slip All living things on God's earth excrete.

Castle Not on my head. If a bird comes close to me, even a little pip with a twitter, I'll whack it with my shovel.

Slip Whoreson. You're jealous 'cause they're up high and you're down here.

Castle Wrote a poem for them, I did. Called it 'The Hateful Bastards'.

These pieces of feathery globs in the sky
They shit as they fly, and no one asks why.
Take a stick when it's dark and find where they roost
Then whack off their heads and suck out their bloost.

Slip Their bloost?

Castle That's their blood when I need it to rhyme.

Slip You can't just make up a word. There's laws attached. They could hang you. (*Slip quits working and looks for Asquith.*) I think he's in the North Field. Let's have a break. Breathe the air.

Castle Don't like the air. Birds fly in it.

Castle and Jayfort stop working.

Slip Can't say I miss the city. Sure miss the ships, though.

Castle Rather be in Deptford right now. And if we hadn't joined in on that ruckus, that's where we'd be.

Slip You're to blame for that! 'Burn the ship!' 'Burn the ship!' Whose voice was that then, clear as a bell?

Castle (*calls*) 'Burn the ship!'

Slip Lucky we weren't hanged.

Castle What a sight, eh?

Slip I made her deck.

Castle And you could hear her squealing in the flames.

Castle lets out a bizarre and frightening scream of the wood burning. The other men duck.

Slip Shhh!

Castle That's how green wood screams.

Slip Give us some bread then.

Jayfort has taken a piece of bread from his coat. He splits it and hands each of his friends a piece.

Castle Up at night with the hunger. I'm near to quit already.

Slip How far is near to?

Castle measures the distance with his arms.

Castle 'Bout that far.

Slip Can't quit. Where'd you go? Can't go back to London. Too hot. Not just us shipbuilders. Strikes with the weavers, merchant seamen. Coal heavers, too.

Jayfort finishes his bread, begins to do some sort of subtle foot work, barely moving, but with precision. The other two men watch as they talk.

Castle (*to Jayfort*) Don't talk much, do you? Cook? Servant? (*Beat.*) Brickledolup?

Slip That's not a word.

Jayfort Sailor. *The Royal Dane.*

Castle and Slip whistle their approval at the same time.

Slip That's a damn good ship. Sugar run?

Jayfort London–Jamaica. Seven years.

Castle You born with the sugar?

Jayfort Father's from Guinea. Me, I'm born in London.

Slip Then why'd you leave?

Jayfort ignores them and continues. Slip mimics his footwork.

I don't know this dance. It's not some magic that's going to turn us into frogs? (*Sings.*) Let's all go a frogging, frogging, let's all go –

Slip looks over to Castle and makes a gesture of insanity. In doing so he accidentally bumps into Jayfort. Jayfort reflexively pulls back his arm ready to strike Slip.

Christ . . .

He begins his footwork again. Castle and Slip watch.

Castle You jump about like a sparrow. Running from the city like us, huh? (*Beat.*) Whose head did *you* shit on?

Jayfort ignores them, continues his footwork.

SCENE THREE

The five villagers, including Ellen, Hesp's mother, are discussing the latest proposal to have their village moved, in what serves for an outdoors meeting place. Hesp stands outside the discussion. Villager One/Lonoff, speaks his words as though they made sense.

Villager Four/Algren He gave us blankets last winter. There's a point. And the winter before.

Villager Three Sent word when my baby died. Sent word when my cow died, too.

Villager Two He sent a basket of jam when I was sick. I say we do what Lord Heywood asks and move.

Villager Three At least he's offered to buy up our lease. More than most lords do. It's fair enough. It's money.

Villager Four/Algren Money's no pull with the old ones. They won't budge.

Villager Two Well, he's got my love, Lord Heywood has. I'd let him use the stick on me if he wanted.

Villager One/Lonoff Worms. Worms and friends stay. Sleep leaves the dark. Not men. Stay. Stay.

Villager Two Why you want to stay? Your house stinks, pig. You don't bother to piss outside.

Villager Three I think I'd like a new house. Forget where I was born. (*Sings.*)

When I was just a little lad
I danced among the corn
And the sky was blue as my mothers legs,
When she was bent and worn.

Villager Four/Algren But there's another point: mothers. Let's make a list. I'll write the points down. This spot is where we come from. Generations of –

Villager Three (*interrupts*) Nah, you were born in the stables thirty miles out.

Villager One/Lonoff Holly is white. So is sand. Close your hand. Live. Live.

Villager Three And die here? That what you want? Of consumption from damp walls?

Villager Four/Algren Let's write down the good points and the bad points.

Villager Two Oh, stuff your points up your arse, braggart. We know you can write. I say let's go now and tell him we'll move.

Ellen Oh stop it. I've said it before: let's wait and see. We've got some time. They have to shift the water before anything else.

Villager Two That'll take that fancy gardener ages.

Ellen He's not a gardener: he's a 'landscape artist'.

Titters all around.

And he's brother to the famous Capability Brown.

Villager Three (*chants*)
There once was a man named Brown
Who planned to pull up the town

Villager Two (*chants*)
But he fell in his lake
With hardly a wake,

Ellen (*chants*)
With a fish in his throat he did drown.

Villager Two Is this gardener pretty? What's his name?

Villager Three Asquith Brown.

Villagers all try out variations of the name of 'Asquith'.

Villager Four/Algren Sounds like a weed. I should write it down.

Ellen He's brought in the diggers. They're taking work we could use. The more they work, the less we'll eat.

Villager One/Lonoff Eat grass. Stir wood. Scrape, scrape. Little insects in the eyes. That's a cattle's pride.

Villager Four/Algren There's another point. (*writing*) Pride. For pride's the poor man's bread.

All Villagers (*interrupt*) Oh shut up, idiot. I'm going home. Enough of this. (*etc*)

Villager Three

We're stopped between castle and kennel
Happy we're neither lord nor his turd
But here come the pick axe and shovel
And we're as hapless as twittering bird, bird, bird –

As they exit, the villagers all join in:

All Villagers

But here come the pick axe and shovel
And we're as hapless as twittering birds.

Only Ellen and Hesp, remain behind. They begin to collect firewood.

Hesp Mother, you speak too loud. Your face gets red, just like the men. You embarrass me.

Ellen I embarrass myself. Heats up the back of my knees.

Hesp They're going to turn that river. Bring it down across the valley, and then off into the woods. And they're moving the hills. It's like God's come back to make a change here and there.

Ellen Now your face is red.

Hesp They've brought in a regiment to do the digging. Soldiers all over the grounds, and each one with a shovel.

Ellen (*playing along with Hesp's dreamy tone*) Shovelling.

Hesp Straining.

Ellen Shovelling. In and out. In and out.

Hesp Sweating . . .

Ellen, talking like a soldier, uses one of the pieces of firewood as an erection. At first Hesp does not notice.

All night the sounds of mud and steel, lonely and sweet and cold.

Ellen pokes Hesp with the wood from behind.

Ellen Hey, little lass. I'm having trouble with my shovel.

Hesp Mother!

Ellen pokes her again, Hesp laughs.

Ellen I've got a stick so dry it just might crack in two if I don't get some real grease soon.

Ellen makes kissing noises. Hesp grabs the wood away from Ellen.

Hesp That's not what I'm looking for, Mother.

Ellen Ah, well. You missed your turn with Michael Marks. He didn't mind a widower.

Hesp I don't like farmers.

Ellen You're a labourer's daughter.

Hesp They smell of cattle. Then they die. We should get away, Mother.

Ellen Just like your father, you are. Away and off to the colonies The new world. With our little baby girl. My little Bliss.

Hesp She had arms like old spindles, Bliss did. Only ten. I was a grown woman. Why didn't Father take me?

Ellen The two of them, swallowed into that dream without so much as a goodbye to the rest of us. Poof! Into Paradise.

Hesp I want to be like that. Just step on a boat, my back to the land, and sail.

Ellen You weren't made for travelling.

Hesp (*ignoring her*) Sometimes I wake in the night and my tongue's gone thick and it's moving with words I don't know. It chokes me. But I'm not afraid. It's a promise, those words. A promise that cannot break.

Ellen Everything breaks, child. Just give it time.

SCENE FOUR

Scarth and Nutley, two soldiers, are digging. Simone enters carrying her easel and a large canvas. At first she ignores the diggers, who ignore her in return. She crosses the stage looking for Asquith. Finally in exasperation she turns on the diggers.

Simone You.

Scarth and Nutley stop and look at one another, each hoping she is referring to the other.

Either of you, it makes no difference. Set up my easel.

Nutley is pushed forward and makes his hesitant way towards Simone.

Please hurry up.

Nutley, after a quick study of this unfamiliar contraption, sets up the easel, and then steps back. Simone then places her picture on the easel and steps back expectantly.

Well, do you see?

The diggers study the painting.

Scarth Visionary . . .

Nutley Yeah, extraordinarily . . .

Scarth . . . visionary . . .

Simone It's unfinished.

Scarth/Nutley Oh.

Simone The tree! The tree! Don't you see the great oak tree?

The diggers lean forward to have a better look.

Scarth Wonderful likeness.

Nutley Beautifully alike the tree.

Simone No. It's not like the tree. Because that tree has vanished. How can I finish my painting without the tree? Where is it? Where is my tree?!

The two soldiers now scan the landscape and they see what she means.

Nutley It's been.

Scarth Finished off.

At this Simone stops and stares at Scarth. Then she quickly collects her painting and easel and marches off.

Nutley It's been 'finished off'? She didn't take to that, did she?

They stand leaning on their shovels.

Scarth Not very appreciative, her. When a tree's got to go it's got to go. This work is sacrifice. Landscaping. Purpose. I'm a part of this. Blisters on my hands. Heel skin coming off. But there's a larger vision, see?

Nutley Naw. Just work. All I see is mud in my sleep. (*Nutley digs a finger in his ear.*) These days, something in my ear. Not a fly. Little crusts of melody. Something coming our way. (*He listens.*) Can you hear it?

Scarth Don't hear nothing. Your ears are buggered. Think she'll come back to paint?

Nutley That was a bastard to cut up, that tree.

Scarth Elephant tree. Shame, really. Two weeks ago, wasn't it though?

Nutley Slow painter, she is.

SCENE FIVE

Asquith, alone, on his hands and knees, rescuing a dozen small saplings trampled in the night. But most of the small trees are beyond saving.

Asquith Damn. When I find out I'll . . . And so quiet now. Oh. My. Little. Ones. Who has done this to you? Lying down. You were never meant to lie down. You were meant to grow up and up and up until you could slash whole acres out of the sky . . . Yes, I know what Lancelot will say, (*mocking*) 'Not keeping your focus . . . guarding your work . . . eye of the hawk' and all that. Well, you, my brother, may live for a tomorrow when your trees are grown up tall, but a man needs a little spoon of water for a dry throat today.

Suddenly Hesp is standing there, looking at this man down on his knees.

Hesp Are you hurt, sir?

Asquith hurriedly gets to his feet. He is embarrassed at being overheard but covers it.

Asquith Do you know anything about this? Someone has broken into the nursery and destroyed a number of my saplings.

Hesp I know nothing about it, sir. I'm –

Asquith (*interrupts. Holds out a small sapling*) Look at this. *Pinus virginiana*. For weeks this single tree sailed the cold, killing waters, its roots encased in its native Virginian soil. Half of them died on the voyage. But this one made it. Only to be trampled on English soil . . . Why? (*He picks up another sapling.*) *Pinus rigida*. Why would someone . . . And there, *Pinus umbra*. That severed one, *Pinus laricio*. Here, smell the needles.

He crushes some of the needles between his fingers and Hesp hesitantly smells them.

The smell of the new world.

Hesp You're Mr Asquith Brown, are you not?

Asquith is distracted.

I live with my mother in the village.

Asquith The village that does not want to move.

Hesp It's the old ones. They're stubborn. Me, I think I'd like a change –

Asquith (*interrupts*) Look, look. From this point of view you see nothing. But when I'm done there will be gently rising hills. Fields that pretend to go on forever. A river that bends like a living animal. How would you like to stand here and experience that?

Hesp That would be beautif –

Asquith (*interrupts*) Not if half way across the park your eye got caught and twisted up on half-a-dozen murky, squatting structures. And truth be told, when the wind isn't right, there is a smell that Lord Heywood finds offensive. I'm drawing up the plans for the new village. I won't be inconsiderate; you'll have thick walls.

Hesp Thank you, sir.

Asquith (*regarding her for the first time*) Why are you out here, alone, so early? Does your husband not mind?

She notices a sapling and picks it up.

Hesp My husband is dead seven years now. Black fever. This one is not broken.

Asquith Oh . . . Then you may have it.

Hesp Is this one from across the waters?

Asquith *Pinus sylvestris*. From Scotland. (*Pause.*) Not from the new world.

Hesp Your hands are not the hands of a labourer, yet they say your father was a farmer.

Asquith Who says that?

Hesp Just people, sir.

Asquith Well, well . . . So, a batch of my saplings are gone. But we'll make do. Ingenuity here. Fast thinking. Lord Heywood won't need to be bothered.

Hesp Cabbage planter.

Asquith Cabbage . . .?

Hesp That's what they call you, sir.

Asquith Who?

Hesp It's been said. That's all.

Asquith As to my past, my father was a farmer, yes. But Lancelot and I have been to school and made ourselves into gentlemen, and I believe all the more thoroughly so due to the becoming than if we had been born as such. (*Starts to go but turns back.*) Details of the past do not interest me, Miss. If what is behind us is darkness, let it be at our backs, not in our faces.

Asquith exits.

Hesp (*to herself*) My name is Hesp Turner.

SCENE SIX

Leafeater appears. He takes a few leaves out of his pockets as he speaks and fingers them absent-mindedly.

Leafeater With strong ribs. Ribs like trees. That is the child I was. Ash Pidduck was my name. Be still, be still, I was told. And I was still. I was a gentle youth. As a lad I had a grey pony. But I didn't ride him. Instead we walked the woods side by side, my pony dreaming of apples and I dreaming of their hidden core and bright, black seeds. I was hopeful and I danced upon the grass, hirrump, hurrah, hooray. I thought as a man I would rule these grounds, but it was not to be. (*Thinks he hears something.*) What's that? (*Beat.*) Be still, be still, I was told. I was not fit. So I was still. I would be the ground's keeper. Nineteen I was. Guarding the deer from the rabble. And then afterwards. After it happened, the accident. The accident. I went to sea.

Split scene: somewhere else, as Leafeater continues speaking, a small place in the stage begins to open. Leafeater cannot 'see' the small person emerging from a hole in the ground, feet first. First a foot comes out, then another. Bliss is an eleven-year-old, small for her age. She shakes the dirt from her clothes.

Shhh. What's that? Like dancing at the gallows, hirrump hurrah hooray . . . its the sailor's life for . . . the month of May. Months when the dead at sea dare to raise their heads and sickness swirls inside their skulls. Hairless, blue, we pitched the fever overboard. Ireland, the Carolinas, Antigua, Barbados, Boston. Years spent puking down the side of sickly ships. And it never left me alone, no matter where I swam, and that's how it felt: swimming from colony to colony, bulging with spices and tea, with *It* breathing down my neck, whispering sweet nibblings into my ear, hirrump hurrah hooray. A little piece of England trailing me through the other little Englands, swamps of money-making and misery, vistas of riot and religion, all hirrump hurrah hooray and the worry, the gibbering fear that the Africans or Indians would jump us. Oh, the sound of water in my ears. (*Startles.*) Jumping. And all that blood moving, moving through little Englands with sharpened teeth to eat through the hard green forests of each new paradise. And me always me swimming, swimming with *It* gnawing at my back. Ah, there's another.

He picks up a long digging hoe. He breaks it across his knee. At the crack, Bliss looks sharply in his direction, though he does not see her.

This is not a good place to dig.

SCENE SEVEN

Bliss wanders the stage, making a clicking sound as though she is calling to someone or something. Then she disappears.

SCENE EIGHT

Nutley shrieks off-stage. Scarth appears, dragging a sack, followed by Nutley.

Scarth Stop that shrieking!

Nutley Stop making that clicking sound!

Scarth I am not making a clicking sound. It's in your head. You're frightened.

Nutley (*acts this out*) You'd be a mite flustered yourself if you'd squat down in a field to crap and a face is looking up at your bollocks through the dirt.

Scarth Not a face. A skull.

Nutley What's the difference?

Scarth Not a face.

Nutley I shat in its gob. I'll go to hell for it.

Scarth Just pop 'em in a sack and bury them, Mr Brown says. Hush, hush. Some extra tobacco for the two of us.

Nutley I don't smoke. They weren't cold. You notice?

Scarth Don't notice nothing. Told Mr Brown he can count on me.

Nutley Warm almost, like bread. How many you think we dug up?

Scarth Only one skull. That's all. Like the Mister said, just a pauper.

Nutley gingerly takes the bag from Scarth and peers inside.

Nutley Lots of bones. Too many bones for just one skull. Lots of little bones too. (*Nutley reaches in the bag and pulls out a small bone.*)

Scarth Put that back, cosier.

Nutley pulls out another. He taps them gently together.

Nutley Must be lonely down under. No one to touch. You never get your bone kissed. Ping, ping. Not while you're alive.

Scarth I get my bone sucked, more often than you no doubt.

Nutley I don't want to bury them.

He hesitantly kisses the bones, first one, then the other.

Scarth Stop that.

Nutley Man or woman, you think? They're so small.

Scarth I'm not part of this.

Nutley Kiss it.

Scarth No thank you.

Nutley approaches him. Grabs him by the neck.

Nutley Kiss it.

He squashes Scarth's face against the small bone, releases him.

Scarth Bastard!

Nutley My hands are cold. Skin's coming off my feet. Can't get them dry. I piss mud.

The two men stare silently at the small bones in Nutley's hands. Nutley taps the bones together.

Hear that?

Scarth I hear nothing.

Nutley drops his hands and looks out across the landscape.

Nutley Rather be at war.

SCENE NINE

Lights up on Slip, Castle and Jayfort who have been surrounded by the villagers, including Hesp.

Villager Four/Algren Lay down your equipment and refuse to dig.

Villager One/Lonoff Blast, blast. Pig feet knee deep in your sleep. So run, stay. Run!

Ellen Quit or we'll halve you with your very own shovels.

The villagers move closer.

Villager Two (*to Jayfort*) You're a strange one, you are.

Now they all inch towards Jayfort. Jayfort suddenly swings his shovel up between himself and the crowd to protect himself.

Oh. He wants a fight.

Villager One/Lonoff Blast! Blast!

Jayfort No one wants a fight.

Slip If we go, they'll just replace us. That won't help you.

Castle We need the work. You need the work. What can be done?

Ellen Tax them.

All Villagers What?

Ellen Let's tax them. The lord taxes us, we'll tax the diggers. Not much, just a pinch at the end of each month.

Jayfort A pinch is all we get right now. There's nothing left over.

Villager Four/Algren Give us your leftovers, then.

Slip You mean our chips? You don't get chips for digging.

Villager Two What do you mean 'chips'?

Castle Down in London, half the ships that left the docks left under our coats. That's chips.

Jayfort But there's nothing sailing here, see.

Villager Three We get leftovers at the end of each season.

Castle There's nothing but dirt at the end of our day.

Ellen Then there's nothing to make peace with. Come on, you lambs. Let's make them piss off.

Villagers crowd in further.

Jayfort Wait. If we have to go, you'll get nothing.

Castle Yeah. Give us a few weeks. We'll make it fair.

Slip We'll find something we can spare . . . (*to Hesp*) Beautiful lass. To you. I give you my word.

Slip holds out his hand to shake, Hesp just barely touches his hand.

Villager One/Lonoff Oh burn, burn. Serenity.

Ellen We won't give you long.

Villager Two We'll be back. Bastards.

The villagers make up a song.

All Villagers (*sing*)
Although we love our labours
As much as our great neighbours

Villager Two
And we bow when the lord, he shits,

All Villagers (*sing*)
We think its only fair
When our days are worse for wear,

Villager Three
That we have a right to our chips.

The villagers sing the song again, in unison this time. Then they move away. They are startled a moment to hear Jayfort sing as they move away.

Jayfort
We think it's only fair
When our days are worse for wear,

Jayfort, Castle and Slip
That we have a right to our chips.

Castle (*to Jayfort*) You know how to wield that shovel.

Jayfort I know how to protect my own. Shovel, rope, stick –

Jayfort picks up a handful of dirt and throws it after the already departed villagers.

Dirt if that's all I can find.

Castle Maybe we've been working with a murderer all this time, hey, Slip?

Slip still looks dreamily after the villagers, and Hesp.

Slip Hmmm?

Castle That why you left London? Let me see those hands again?

Jayfort holds out his hands to Castle.

Maybe you've got killin' in your bloost. I heard it said.

Jayfort And I heard it said that your kind got straw for bones, that dry, catch fire in the hot of July. Nothing in your heads but celestial slime and you like to eat your thumbs.

Slip Hmmm. You read that in a book?

Castle Thank you very much.

Slip I like books.

Jayfort goes back to work.

Jayfort Nah. But I know how to work.

Slip I couldn't give three fucks for this work. I've seen my mission in a young girl's eyes.

Castle Hardly a girl. A bit worn at the edges. You better watch out. Probably got a turglsnippler under her skirts.

Slip Yeah. We'll need a new word for what she's got to offer.

SCENE TEN

Ellen is hoeing. Villager Four is taking down a letter for her.

Ellen How far have I got?

Villager Four/Algren (*sighs, and quotes*) 'My Dearest Piss Hole Husband.'

Ellen That's right.

Villager Four/Algren Last winter it was 'My Darling Dumpling Husband.'

Ellen I'm not, today, in a dumpling mood. Let's keep it at 'My Dearest Piss Hole Who Up and Left. This is the . . .'

She tallies it up in her mind.

'. . . seventeenth letter I have sent you in almost . . . fifteen years now. The hair on my head is grey. Yours must be too. Is your hair grey on your pudding stick –'

Villager Four/Algren I won't write that. You know I won't.

Ellen All right. Then . . . 'How is little Bliss? She is a woman already years now. Are her buttocks plump?

Villager Four/Algren (*still writing*) Careful . . .

Ellen Her sister Hesp's still are . . . Just like mine . . . Tell Bliss what I always tell you to tell her and it doesn't get any less in my heart . . . They might have the village moved. So when the two of you come back and the house is gone, walk one mile to the east, that's where they say they'll put us. Yours always, Ellen.

Villager Four/Algren To Boston again this time? Or New York?

Ellen No. Send it to Vir . . . gin . . . ia. I like the sound of that place. And a postscript.

Villager Four opens the letter again to add to it.

Ellen I have not fucked another man in all this time.

Villager Four/Algren Lain. (*Writes.*) I have not lain with another man in all this time.

Ellen I know you probably have, but I don't care. You bastard. I want you under my skirt every night, I think about it still. Your tongue between my legs was so – (*Beat.*) – unforgivable and hard.

Villager Four/Algren No. Stop it.

Ellen suddenly grabs Villager Four by the scruff of the neck.

Ellen Like the finger of God.

Villager Four/Algren Never!

Ellen releases Villager Four and turns away , finishing her letter. But Villager Four does not write, he just looks at her.

Ellen (*quietly*) The spring still comes to us, my love. And the rain. The birds have been to wars on other lands, but they bring us. No word.

SCENE ELEVEN

Hesp and Slip talking together. Slip takes a break from work.

Slip On every corner, a different language. Like bits and pieces of Christmas in the air. London. It's worlds in a single city. And I can speak Dutch: *Wat een leuk meid ben je*. And Spanish: *Quiero besarte muchisimo*. And even a strange one, no one knows where it came from –

He makes up a language and it sounds almost 'real'. Hesp laughs. She's impressed despite herself.

Hesp Taught myself to read. Lord Heywood gave each family a book. He gave my mother *Pilgrim's Progress*. And we discovered that we're all stuck in the Slough of Despond. I think the colonies are the –

Slip The Delectable Mountains?

Hesp You've read it too?

Slip Heard it talked about. Maybe I can borrow your book?

Hesp You can read?

Slip No.

Hesp Then what good will a book do you?

Slip I can look at the pages. Touch the pages you've touched.

Hesp That's not reading.

Slip Ah. Words aren't just for reading. They like to be looked at, they like to be touched, for themselves, now and then. Just for the love of it.

Hesp For the love of it. Huh. I don't know. (*Hesp picks up a blade of grass.*)

Slip Do you like to be looked at? (*Beat.*) Do you like to be touched?

Hesp Maybe I do.

Hesp blows a loud noise on the grass. Impressive. Slips picks a blade of grass. He blows. He can't do it. Hesp laughs.

My father taught me. As a child. He could blow so you heard it three miles out. And I'd come running across the fields to bring him home. (*Beat.*) In the mornings he got up early for work while we slept. Every night before I fell asleep I swore I'd get up before he did so he wouldn't be alone. But he always got to the morning before we did, already standing at the door, looking out at the black. My father went away, long before he went away. He just didn't want us to know it. (*Beat.*) Hey, teach me to dance one of those new city dances?

Slip It's not a thing a lady would do. Not the ladies in London anyway.

Hesp Oh.

Slip And you, dear Hesp, are the closest thing to a lady I've seen since I've come to this Dale.

Hesp blows again on the grass, this time an ugly sound.

Hesp Ha. I'm a potato picker. What a lying tongue you have. Say it again. I like it.

Slip You are the closest thing to a lady I've –

Suddenly Asquith appears. He has overheard the last of their conversation. He carries some plans which he has been studying.

Asquith But the ladies in London *do* dance. Not like at the dockyards, either. They wear gowns with glass beads so bright it pains the eyes to look at them. Hold these.

He hands the plans to Slip. He takes Hesp in his arms to dance with her.

May I? Now just relax and follow the flow. Relax. This dance has a more open feel, a sweep . . . That's it . . . Most common dances, the design is too . . . artificial. (*to Slip*) Have you had a read of Burke's *Enquiry into the Origin of Our Ideas of the Sublime and Beautiful*?

Slip Course I have.

Asquith (*to Hesp*) Don't look at your feet, just rest, even while you're moving. (*to Slip*) And what do you think of his inquiry, then?

Slip I think, sir, that it is about one man's ideas . . . of love . . .

Asquith Love? Nonsense. It's about the sublime. Read in conjunction with Hogarth's *Analysis of Beauty*, it might give a man an idea or two.

Slip That's right, sir. And each man has an idea, and each man has a . . . pair of slippers if he is lucky.

Asquith (*amused*) Slippers? I don't think Burke –

Slip (*interrupts*) But most of us aren't lucky, sir . . . and we've only our . . . working shoes . . . and inside those shoes is the idea that (*gaining in confidence*) the foot, that looks hard down into the ground with the bottom of its soul, day after day, knows more than we know with our dirty hearts: that starved beauty would rather kiss an ankle ringed with dirt than suck love on a rich man's thumb.

Asquith Well, well . . . You may not know how to read Burke, my man, but you do know how to fancy. But fancy, alas, is what we are digging up and turning over out here. (*to Hesp*) We must create, shall we say, spaces of grace . . . spaces without fancy. Something new out of the old. For instance, at a distance, this moment might look, to the ignorant or melodramatic mind, like a well-worn story: a gentleman out to seduce a common maid. But take a closer look and one might see new, bold movement in that tired design, such as one finds in the paintings of Claude Lorrain. In his eye, the world stretches into the distance . . . (*back to Hesp*) Just as the body should. That's right. That's nice. Turn, and circle and sweep. No straight lines. A straight line of movement belongs in the mathematician's book. A straight line has no spirit. It's predictable.

They come to a stop. Hesp and Asquith look at one another.

On a straight line, you cannot dream

Slip looks away in disgust.

SCENE TWELVE

Leafeater sits staring into space. He suddenly looks over his shoulder. As he does so Jayfort, carrying a number of shovels, enters. He stops when he sees Leafeater.

Leafeater Turn to the left. Hmm. Now to the right.

Jayfort turns to leave.

I would bet you're from one of the Leeward Islands, perhaps –

Jayfort London.

Leafeater Close. One can tell a lot by the shape of a nose, the slant of the forehead, the space between the eyes – shh! Did you hear that?

Leafeater gets up, looks around, sits down again. He takes a plant from his pocket and eats a leaf from it.

You're a sailor. And black. Now. What about me. My face.

Jayfort Your face.

Leafeater I have one, do I not? Or at least I did, once upon a time before *It* ate at it piece by piece. Maybe it's you, out to eat the rest of me, the beast in a snake's clothing. (*He drops to his belly.*) After my face. (*Pause.*) What do you see? Tell me.

Jayfort That you are white. (*Jayfort puts down the shovels and approaches Leafeater.*) And in the dirt. Are you ill?

Leafeater Keep your distance. I don't want it. I've got my own. Oceans of the damned stuff. Now get down, get down. Like me. And swim. (*Leafeater swims, snake-like.*) I order you. I'm your superior!

Jayfort (*crouches near Leafeater*) I knew a man who thought he was possessed by a demon. A dog, he said. His captain's dog was inside him.

Leafeater stops swimming and is alert.

Leafeater He was your friend? You loved him?

Jayfort He was flogged same as me. We both were sailors. I offered to help him, but he wouldn't have it. A week later, he ate three of his fingers clear off his left hand. I told him, 'Drink this.' It would have calmed him, but he spat at me. A week after that he'd started on his other hand. I asked him why he'd devour his own flesh, but he wouldn't tell me. He said a black man could not know a white man. So I left him to it. I watched him eat himself until he went mad and was thrown overboard. But he was wrong. I knew him better than he knew me. He only knew he was white because of me. Without me, he would have disappeared.

Jayfort collects up the shovels. Leafeater watches him, motionless.

You're right. I'm a sailor. I'm black. But the rest of it. I leave you to it.

Leafeater jumps up and strikes the pose of a 'superior'.

Leafeater But I was a sailor once. We are equals then, you and I? As God said to himself.

Jayfort (*turns back toward Leafeater, who retreats slightly*) Equals? I've not seen you round Seven Dials, and I know all there, specially the mad. An artist once asked my master if he might capture my likeness in a painting – a page boy with enormous round eyes. I stood for him in his studio two or three times. Open your eyes, he shouted.

Leafeater Open your eyes, damn you!

Jayfort I did. And I ran off to sea.

SCENE THIRTEEN

Simone paints. A small table, with tea, is close by. Castle is planting a sapling elsewhere. He keeps slipping in the mud.

Simone Could you please stop splashing about in the mud? You're distracting me.

Castle stops planting. He just stands and looks at her. She paints on, absorbed. He inches closer. Closer. He can see what's on the tea tray now.

What do you want?

Castle Just. Having a. Look.

Simone You'll have to come around this side for a 'look'.

Castle At the biscuits. Nice ones, those.

Simone Have one then. I've probably fed half the regiment by now.

Castle inches closer. Takes one biscuit daintily. Chews. Now he studies her painting.

Must you chew like a horse?

Castle Sorry, ma'am. Mouth's dry.

Simone Have some tea, then.

Castle pours a little tea. Drinks it. Simone studies a colour.

There's something wrong with the sky. It's too . . . blue.

Castle Looks a good sky to me. None of those nasty birds in it.

Simone Every man, no matter his station, should have an affinity for birds. They represent freedom, the unrestricted flights of the imagination. (*She concentrates again on her work.*)

Castle Birds are known as nelumpfuddlian creatures. Though some. Ancient science men. Called them twackenwickets.

Simone (*not really listening*) Oh?

Castle The movements of their wings, those little tiny bones, called gristhilibits.

Simone Be quiet now. I'm working.

Castle They have twelve gristhilibits per wing.

Simone Dear man. You may think, if that is a function that's possible for you, that I am simply a useless, and most likely impoverished, Lady of the Dales who dabbles in artistry, and therefore you have a right to mock me. I am, however, a third cousin of Lord Heywood's, and he will pay me generously for these half-dozen portraits of his land. Or what his land was before you started digging. I am doing a service here. My hand is remembering this landscape in a way the mind never will.

Castle Just one wee question.

Simone I am trying to work.

Castle What's that. In the background?

Simone That's a peasant.

Castle Can't hardly tell. Looks like a chicken. Upside down.

Simone turns to glare at him, then continues.

I like chickens. Though this one looks bent and crippled.

Simone My peasant represents the fruits of honest labour, a body at one with the natural world.

Castle Oh. Then, why not put him. Right up here at. The front.

Simone Because he didn't pay for this painting. He's lucky he makes an appearance at all.

Castle So that's how things. Are. In the paintings. Ma'am?

Castle moves off a little. He takes another biscuit.

Simone It's not about how things are. It's about how we would like them to be.

Castle I see.

Simone No. You don't. Here. Let me show you.

Simone stands behind him and puts her hands over his eyes.

Now. See things as you would like them to be. (*Beat.*) Well. What do you see?

Castle is quiet a moment.

Castle Nothing. Just dark.

Simone Oh, relax. (*She massages his eyes a bit roughly.*) Keep looking . . .

Castle I can't with your hands on my eyes.

Simone Now. What do you see?

Castle More of the same. Dark.

Simone Damn it. Imagine something. Imagine a . . . boat . . . and a big blue ocean.

Castle No . . . no . . . Yes! There it is. A little boat. A little green boat. And me. I'm sailing in it. Christ.

The sun's as big as a lake above me. And I got a smile on my face. And . . . and down below in the water I hear a voice calling to me . . . sweetly, sweetly. A woman's voice. And she rises up out of the water. Naked. Completely.

Simone drops her hands but Castle keeps his eyes closed.

Simone That's enough.

Castle And she floats. She floats. Towards. Me! Closer, closer, wet and glimmering and her delicate hand reaches out and grabs ahold of my pindaflipster.

Simone abruptly returns to her painting. Then he opens his eyes.

Got no use for your kind of seeing, Missus. When I open my eyes, it's gone.

SCENE FOURTEEN

Bliss is still wandering and looking. Then she 'sees' the public, the dead who do not want her to leave them, even for a little while.

Bliss No. Not yet. Not yet. I have business first. My teeth hurt. Thrice a beetle said, 'Get up, get up.' In my grave I was swimming. I was swimming. Then a mole pissed in my hand but still I couldn't wake. Then there were soldiers digging in the dirt and I woke up. (*Beat.*) I have business. I won't go back in my hole. You can stay and rest on your pillows stuffed with grubs that turn their lullabies but I have to. I have to. I. (*distracted*) There was something he said but it was only. Water. Something he did and it made a. Chain. In my dark I was swimming, and calling. Calling and swimming.

The fins of fish pricked hard in my breast. (*to public again*) No. I won't come back to my grave. Not yet. I must find. I must find him. Because I can't remember . . . (*loud*) Shhh. God damn you. We're dead. Accept it. (*quiet again*) When I am done, then I will come back and lie down again with you and I will gather in my breast your last words of bitter harvest, circling under the earth, and I will hear you. (*Beat.*) I will hear you. Out.

SCENE FIFTEEN

Asquith and Hesp stand together. He has a variety of fine tools in a wooden box.

Asquith That is a puffer. This, a slasher, and a small billhook. And next to it, an aphis brush. May I show you? It is in effect a pair of brushes on tongues – (*He takes her hand and demonstrates on one of her fingers, sliding the tool across her fingers.*) – allowing the brushes to clear both sides of a leaf or stem simultaneously. So that it can breathe free.

She now pulls her hands away, as though embarrassed.

Hesp A leaf or stem. Such things are, by their nature, beautiful.

Asquith I'm sorry. I didn't mean to . . .

Hesp It is your hands, Mr Asquith, which are beautiful.

Asquith Are they?

Hesp Yes. Can you not see it?

Asquith Surely it is your own hands which are –

Hesp (*interrupts*) These hands, Mr Asquith? Ha. Look at them. (*She holds out her hands for his closer inspection.*)

Across the left palm, a blade from cutting meat. The right hand, nasty, isn't it? My father and I were slaughtering when I was twelve and the pig took my thumb. My mother says our hands, our bodies even, are the history of insults that have been inflicted against them.

Asquith takes her two hands in his and studies them.

Asquith But then our bodies must therefore also be the culmination of pleasures that have been inflicted upon them.

Hesp My hands were not ruined through pleasure, sir.

Asquith Goodness, you truly are a woman with a. Reflective mind.

Asquith awkwardly takes into his mouth as much of her hand as he can manage. Hesp does not resist.

Hesp If I closed my eyes I might imagine . . .

Asquith gently takes her hand from his mouth. She smiles at him. Then she slaps him. He steps back.

I think that is called for when a gentleman puts a woman's fingers in his mouth, be she only a cattle rag.

Asquith I'm sorry. I thought you – I do not know how to act. To a woman. I do not have a. Wife.

Hesp I like the sound of your voice, Mr Brown. But not the sound of lies. A man of your experience, your knowledge –

Asquith (*interrupts*) I know grass. I know hills. I can touch the bark of a tree and know its age. I can close my eyes and smell a crushed leaf and tell you what branch it fell from. I have not taken a wife because I have not met a woman who could change me.

Hesp And how would you like to be changed, sir?

Asquith I do not know. I would expect her to bring me that knowledge. (*Beat.*) Look. Look out at all of this. I can change this landscape. Alone, I cannot alter who I am. (*Beat.*) Why do you come here?

Hesp does not answer but looks away.

Hesp My father sailed to the colonies over fifteen years ago, Mr Asquith. Just up and left. I suppose he wanted a change. But not on the inside. He wanted a change of place. He took my little sister, too. If there are persons in this world that I despise, it is them. For leaving me behind.

Asquith There is as much death and disease abroad as –

Hesp (*interrupts*) But there is so much. Space. Space. New space. One could turn and turn and run blindly in any direction and bump into nothing but wild animals.

Asquith One day, when my name is better known, I too might travel. Across the sea. I do not intend to stay here, as my brother does, waiting decades for these landscapes to reach maturity. Just for a little while, I would like to sit down on old hills and look at my shoes, instead of at the distance.

Hesp Perhaps you could find a place where you could do both.

Asquith Do you think so? My brother would say that to desire both leads to indecision, poor planting. And he'd be right. There is nothing that he says that is not right. And yet the more I speak of his brilliant transformation of this land, the less I am transformed.

Hesp Then speak less. My father used to say that too much talk brings crows and in their wings they'll carry swords.

Asquith Meaning?

Hesp (*laughing*) I have no idea.

Asquith Hmmm. And if I went across the sea, what would you give to go with me?

Hesp Sir, you make fun of my poverty.

Asquith Answer me.

Hesp Well, then, to take me with you, I would give you exactly half.

Asquith Fair enough.

Hesp Of everything I'll never own.

SCENE SIXTEEN

Slip, Jayfort and Castle crouch together. It is night.

Jayfort Best to blacken your faces.

Castle Blacken?

Jayfort Don't need two great full moons following me around; give the game away.

Slip Following you? Thought we were in this together!

Castle It's dark enough already.

Jayfort All the more reason. You'll stand out like the death's head. Here, use this. It's polish.

Jayfort produces a small pot of black polish.

Slip Don't like it.

Castle Me neither.

Jayfort You'll like it less when they wipe that whiteness off your faces with a ball or two.

Castle My face might save me, though. Who are they more likely to shoot?

Slip Good point.

Jayfort I thought we were in this together.

Castle Yeah, but, you know . . . I never been black before.

Slip Nor have I.

Jayfort Listen to me: either you go black or I go home.

Slip and Castle consider this, then reluctantly apply the polish to their faces. They purposely miss a few places, which Jayfort touches up as they continue to speak.

Slip But you just don't know what might happen.

Jayfort Yeah, I do: exotic plants, expensive plants. There for the taking. For the selling. And then we can eat. And if we're careful, just take a few, they'll never notice . . .

Finally they are all 'blacked up'.

Slip/Castle Satisfied?

Jayfort Might save your life. Brothers of mine.

Nutley and Scarth appear. They are on patrol. They stop and lean on their rifles.

Scarth Bosket!

Nutley Shut up, you. Babble like a magpie.

Scarth That's a gardening word, that is.

Nutley Meaning?

Scarth I don't rightly know, but I'm weasured, done.

Nutley Yeah. Guarding shrubs. Defending the country. Side.

Scarth Gard-en-ing.

Nutley Mmm.

Scarth But, I'm picking up a thing or two. Dibbles. Pruning knife. A digging shoe. Gardening things. Gardening ideas.

Nutley Why?

Scarth Soldiering isn't where I'm going to stop for the rest of my life. London's gardens call for Capability Scarth.

Nutley Bet London can hardly wait.

Nutley has taken from his pocket two small bones. He knocks them together, gently.

Scarth I've been watching this Brown, and though he's not an army man, he thinks in a soldiering way. Damn it. You were supposed to bury those things. If the Mister catches you

Nutley In a bag, hid them under my cot. Why weren't they in the graveyard?

Scarth If you get us – Look. I'm here to finish this job. I'm watching, I'm learning. It's all strategy and opening up clear lines of fire. All the old gardens with their walls and ditches and terraces – ramparts, ravelins, parterres, and what have you – that's all defences, that is; and Brown's lark is just a simple change of venue: he gets rid of the fort and plants a battlefield.

They are startled by Jayfort, Slip and Castle, who suddenly appear, having tried to sneak past. Scarth and Nutley, terribly frightened, confront the trespassers, Scarth with his rifle, Nutley with the two bones.

Nutley Who? Who?

Scarth Stop!

Nutley Who? Who?

Jayfort, Slip and Castle come forward, their arms raised. The two sides study one another.

Slip The North Field diggers.

Scarth Three blackies?

Castle The owl and the bone man.

Scarth Put those away, you triptoe.

Nutley quickly does so and picks up his gun.

Castle Only he's black.

Scarth Well, can't sell the two of you. Not what's wanted. Now, as for you –

Scarth moves to grab Jayfort, but Jayfort grabs Scarth's arm and forces it behind his back in a painful half-nelson. With his other arm he grabs Scarth's lower jaw. Nutley brings his rifle up to Jayfort's neck. Jayfort does not let go.

Castle Jayfort doesn't like to be touched.

Nutley Why's that? How can you live, then?

Jayfort Got to go. Backwards. Way back. Just far enough.

Jayfort releases Scarth. Nutley lowers the gun.

Then I'll make in these hands a different will, another job one day.

Nutley We're . . . we're just soldiers.

Slip Mud-movers, you mean. Like us.

Scarth You're trespassing. Can't let you spoil this work.

Castle Least we ain't been grave-robbing.

Leafeater enters and creeps up behind the soldiers. Nobody sees him.

Scarth I could kill you. I've killed before.

Jayfort Killed innocent men looking for a means to buy food? Proud, are you?

Suddenly Jayfort springs at Nutley, knocking him over, just as Leafeater is about to grab him. The other men recoil from Leafeater, who now crouches in their midst.

Leafeater Give me those bones.

Nutley Oh, help. Don't touch me.

Leafeater They bite when you least expect it. Hirrump, hurrah, hooray!

Scarth points his gun but Leafeater seems oblivious to it.

Scarth Who are you?

Jayfort He's been snooping around here for weeks.

Castle A green loon –

At this Leafeater advances towards Castle. All the men retreat in fear.

Leafeater Hirrump!

Jayfort Running from –

Leafeater Swimming. I am swimming and I can't stop. (*to Jayfort*) I see a boat in your eyes. Take me away.

Jayfort Sorry. I'm done with the ships. It's all dry land for me.

Leafeater But the winds are just right. Take me away.

Scarth Evil green spirit, he is. Might just poison the lot of us.

Leafeater Give me the bones.

Nutley No! Never.

Leafeater digs in his many pockets and finds a coin. Leafeater holds out his hands for Nutley's bones.

But I'm hungry. Going to miss them. When you knock them together, ding, ding, dong.

Leafeater takes the bones and hides them in his pockets.

Leafeater I must go. Beware. Take care. The moon burns a hole in your back as you walk.

Leafeater exits. The men stand bewildered. After a moment, Castle takes the black polish from his pocket and holds it up for Nutley and Scarth to see.

Castle Soldiers of England, fancy putting a bit of this on your faces?

SCENE SEVENTEEN

Bliss alone on stage. She moves about the grounds. She is still looking for something.

Bliss Where. Where. (*She whistles softly, as if calling for something.*) Where are you? Where are you? You'll tell me.

SCENE EIGHTEEN

Hesp and Ellen are planting potatoes.

Ellen Rattle, rattle. A plate of stones. He's nothing to get fat on.

Hesp He's got near over a hundred men digging now. He has to be tough. It's his job.

Ellen And mine is to feed the both of us.

Hesp Don't you want something better for me? I've lost a husband, mother. You know yourself what that's like. And I'm still young.

Ellen He's got no plans for you past these fields. He won't take you with him.

Hesp He might.

Ellen He won't.

Hesp Stranger things have happened. He plans to go abroad.

Ellen Not with you. Once he's had you, he'll drop you. I've seen if before. Better not give in.

Hesp stops digging. She stands over her mother.

Hesp You're jealous.

Ellen Close your trap, woman.

Hesp You, you've nothing but a husk between your legs. Dried up the day Father left you. Well I didn't dry up, Mother.

Ellen Ha.

Hesp Each morning I wake my bed is wet. I'm still alive inside. I could fill a mug a day from between my legs. That's how much.

Ellen Shut up.

Hesp That's how much I . . . Why can't you hope the best for me? You've no idea what it's like. I want.

Ellen Stop it.

Hesp I want to be choked with it. I want to break. There is not a thing on God's earth like it when you're torn down the middle, rent into a hundred shining pieces –

Ellen grabs her daughter threateningly.

Ellen I've no idea? A husk? That what you think? Because I'm old? For every mug you've filled, my daughter, I've filled a bucket. But I don't whine and squawk about it. I work. I rake the fields. I make your home. Pphhh. You're not the first woman to go without. Won't be the last. Here.

She releases Hesp, slapping a potato into Hesp's hands.

Plug that between your legs and get to work.

Ellen goes back to work. Hesp stands holding the potato.

SCENE NINETEEN

Jayfort, Castle, Slip and Asquith stand around a fire warming their hands, taking a break.

Asquith The new hills are up. Just have to finish the second bend for the waters. Damn water. I love her. Hear how she pushes at the sluice at night? Oh, but she's eager . . .

The diggers are silent.

Lord Heywood's back from his travels. I've asked him to raise the rations. 'When the North Field is done,' he says. I do what I can.

Castle We thank you, sir.

Asquith gets out some tobacco, hands it to Castle to pass around.

Asquith Go on. Have a smoke, the lot of you.

The men are surprised, and take the tobacco.

And a swig. Or two.

He takes a swig himself, then passes around a small flask. The men drink and mutter thank-yous, Asquith sniffs at the fire.

Sometimes I long for the smell of the cottage hearth. The small, damp places of my youth. But for years now I move among lords and ladies. I've quite forgotten how to. Relate. To men like yourselves. Let alone to women. I know you have. Your customs. (*Beat.*) For instance. What might your custom be to court a woman . . . from the village?

The men look at him with suspicion, but are silent.

What must a man do to arouse the. Interest. Of a common woman? (*to Castle*) You there. Answer me.

Castle Me? Well, sir. If I were you I'd just grab her by the skirt and –

Asquith (*interrupts*) No, no. If I were you.

Castle If you were me, well, then I'd just talk to her. And when she laughed, I'd kiss her.

Jayfort and Slip snigger.

Asquith What if I can't make her laugh?

Slip Tell her you respect her virtue, that'll make her laugh.

Asquith Problem is. Well. Well. To be frank, I have only lain with whores. And of course I never kissed them on the mouth. I am at a loss as to how to seduce a. Common woman.

Slip Have you read Hogarth's *Blather and Seduction Through a Gentleman's Socks*? Might give you a few ideas.

Castle Truth be told, it's all in the Niagitherian Thrust: that's a book word for the kiss. Listen, you slobber in her mouth and she'll quit you. You hard-bite her tongue and she'll kick you. The tongue. It's a little. Shovel. You open her lips and you dig a little, then a little more till she's wide open, then you go in deep for that little worm at the back of her throat that makes her sing.

Asquith Well.

Asquith turns to Jayfort.

Jayfort Nah. You don't dig with your tongue. Your tongue. It's a key and you put it in her mouth and turn it like a piece of silver till it opens the lock. And you'll know when you've opened the lock by the click of her teeth against your own. And if she pulls back, turn the key the other way and draw her to you, wind her back to your breast and breathe. Don't forget to breathe because the water's going to rise, spill down your chins and it's ocean, ocean as you never tasted in all your life.

Asquith Oh.

They all turn to Slip, who answers with barely concealed menace.

Slip I just do this.

He clears his throat, gathering phlegm; he makes a real effort at it. He shoots the phlegm ball into the air.

Straight into her mouth. She never forgets me.

Asquith takes a hard swig from his flask.

Asquith Teach me.

The men are silent.

Teach me how to . . . to make her willing. I must not fail.

Slip Hesp. That's who you want, sir. Hesp Turner.

Asquith Yes.

Slip She's a good woman. She can read. Smart, too.

Asquith I'm aware of her qualities. (*Beat.*) Teach me.

Slip Okay. Let's teach him. About the kiss. *The* kiss. The –

Castle – Niagitherian Thrust.

Slip Right. Now. Open your mouth. Please.

Asquith What?

Slip Open you mouth. (*Beat.*) Sir.

Asquith opens his mouth. The three men crowd around.

Jayfort Stick it out.

Castle Go on.

Jayfort Let's have it.

Asquith does so, hesitantly extending his tongue.

Slip Now follow my finger with your tongue.

Slip moves his finger up and down, left to right, and Asquith follows with his tongue. Slip jiggles his finger., Asquith follows. Slip makes circles with his finger. Asquith follows. Then Asquith quits.

Asquith It feels. Unnatural.

Slip Hesp has got brains in her head, sir. She won't be used.

Asquith In my experience, dear man, all of us are to be used. At a price.

Slip Yes. You're right. At a price, sir. Give me a piece of silver and I'll teach you how it's really done. What you want to learn.

Asquith only hesitates a moment.

Asquith All right.

He takes a coin from his pocket. Slip reaches for it, but Asquith holds it back.

After I have my information.

Slip Ready then?

Asquith If you tell me exactly, I could write it down –

Slip (*interrupts*) Can't. It's not meant to be read. It's all right, sir. Trust me. Jayfort, Castle. Send him to me. (*to Asquith's uncertainty*) First you've got to be 'sent', sir.

With a swift movement, Jayfort and Castle push Asquith at Slip. Slip takes Asquith in his arms and kisses him full and long on the mouth, but at the end of the kiss, he hurts him. Asquith cries out in pain. No one moves. Stunned, Asquith wipes the blood from his mouth as he backs away. He stares at Slip. Then the others. He is both afraid and hurt.

(*uncertain himself now*) That's about how it goes. (*Beat.*) Sir.

Asquith Heathens . .

Asquith moves to leave, but then stops. He stares at the three silent men. Then Asquith tosses Slip the coin. Slip catches the coin in the air, and freezes. Asquith exits. Castle and Jayfort look at Slip's raised hand, in which the coin hides. Slip lowers his hand and then slowly opens it to reveal the piece of silver. Already we hear Hesp's song in the distance.

SCENE TWENTY

Hesp is sleep-walking over the countryside. She is in her nightdress and her feet are bare. She does some simple dance steps and turns.

Hesp (*sings*)
I am a lady from Boston town, my skin as white as ice
I sleep on silk and bathe in tea, my pillows filled with spice

I'll not marry, I'll be a grand whore and read and dance and learn
and my bed mates they'll be friends to the king
and all of the city for me will yearn

Bliss 'appears' as if from nowhere. She follows behind Hesp, copying the movements and turns Hesp is making.

Bliss (*sings*)
And my bed-mates they'll be friends of the king
And all the city for me will yearn

Hesp begins to 'hear' this echo, and when she turns, she comes face to face with Bliss.

And all the city for me will burn

They stare at one another.

Your feet are cold.

Hesp looks at her feet.

Hesp I can't feel my feet.

Bliss That's because you're asleep.

Hesp I'm taking a walk.

Bliss In your sleep.

Hesp In *your* sleep.

Bliss I'm not asleep.

Hesp Then I've made you up. See? I could choke you and wake up and there would be no murder.

Bliss You didn't make me. But you could choke me and wake up and there would be no murder. Because I am not here.

Hesp touches the girl's arm.

Hesp Your flesh is real enough. Don't I know your face? No. Who are you?

Bliss I am not here.

Hesp Then we are the same, you and I. When I'm awake, it seems I am not. Here either. I cannot. I cannot make. A river bend. I cannot. Move a hill. I cannot ask men to dig and they dig. Such powerful magic. I would kill for it. So I sleep. And when I sleep I am not hungry and my feet are strong and I can climb trees and houses. I can touch anyone I wish to touch. I can open the trousers of any man. I can lift up my skirts and the lord kneels to lick me. I can say yes, yes, and crystal shatters in the manor. I can say go to hell and soldiers lower their guns.

Bliss Never liked sleep when I was a child. (*Beat.*) I have not slept for fifteen years.

Hesp You are lying.

Bliss You are dreaming. And I am dead.

Hesp Oh. Well. I don't mind. What do you want to do, then?

Bliss Follow the leader.

Hesp I used to do that with my sister, long ago.

Bliss Then let's play.

Hesp I've never played with a dead girl before.

Bliss Your missing out, then.

Bliss turns away and does a slightly complicated step that Hesp must follow. Hesp does, and after a moment of awkwardness, she does it well. Bliss does another and Hesp follows. Bliss sings, and Hesp echoes her.

I am a lady from underground, my skin as white as death
I cannot rest, I cannot sleep, since a magpie stole my breath.

Hesp/Bliss
I cannot rest, I cannot sleep, since a magpie stole my breath.

SCENE TWENTY-ONE

Jayfort is doing his footwork, alone.

Jayfort The head of our ship was an Englishman. He was a fair captain. I said, 'Teach me to read.' He hit me. The next day he complimented me on my cooking. I said, 'Teach me to read.' He hit me again.

Split scene: elsewhere, Asquith stands before the villagers. Scarth and Nutley accompany Asquith. They carry their rifles.

Asquith Thievery of tools and plants. Destruction of young trees.

A giggle comes from the group of villagers.

Jayfort A few days later the captain lay dying, rotting with blueheel fever. I knew the cure. He said, 'Help me.' I said, 'Teach me to read.'

Asquith These are crimes.

Jayfort This time he didn't hit me. He said 'Bring me the book.'

Asquith The law is the law, and Lord Heywood will discover the culprits.

Jayfort And then for months, years, he taught me the book.

Asquith I am his servant.

Jayfort He taught me to read the words. And these words taught me. Some kind of sense.

Asquith I will put an end to this violence against property.

Jayfort All of it in another language than my own. And yet the words, they lodged in my mind. John Milton's words.

Asquith Where are my tools?

Jayfort And these words took up a new space inside me.

Asquith Do you hear what I'm saying?

Jayfort The ocean. The winds. The butchering. The tea.

Asquith I want my tools back. Or.

Scarth One like this?

He takes a pruning knife from beneath his coat. Asquith is bewildered. It is one of the stolen tools.

Jayfort The paradise. The illness. The gifts.

Asquith Yes. That one. Where did you . . . ah, it's the one I gave you.

Jayfort The gods. The trades. The abandon. The silk.

Asquith (*turns back to the villagers*) What have you to say?

Jayfort The sighs. The exchange. The salt. The flesh.

Scarth No, you didn't give me this knife.

Jayfort The navigation: Bengal, Senegal, Mosquito Coast.

Asquith What?

Jayfort Bermuda, Bahamas, Bombay, Surat.

Asquith Understand my meaning –

Jayfort The calico. The flogging. The wealth. The tea. The words.

Asquith – this has gone too far.

Jayfort The words were the alchemy that would build the empires that we would serve. How could I then have an idea that could be outside of this?

Asquith Therefore, if any man or woman does not agree to sell their lease within a fortnight –

Jayfort And then in this book I found something unimaginable.

Jayfort stops his foot work.

Asquith – then they will face the road with nothing.

Villagers (*chanting quietly*)
Venison, venison, God won't save us.
Venison, venison, he went to Barbados.

Asquith The old village will be removed, whether you like it or not.

Villagers
Venison, venison, dance on the gallows.

Asquith Lord Heywood is bringing in more soldiers to dig. So beware.

Jayfort In his book, I found something I could use –

Villagers
Venison, venison, the world before us.

Jayfort (*quoting Milton*)
To overcome in battle, and subdue
Nations, and bring home spoils with infinite
Manslaughter, shall be held the highest pitch
Of human glory –

Villagers
Venison, venison, the world before us.

Jayfort – and for glory done
Of triumph, to be styl'd great conquerors,
Patrons of mankind, gods, and sons of gods
Destroyers rightlier call'd and plagues of men.
Thus fame shall be achiev'd, renown on Earth, (*Beat.*)
And what most merits fame in silence hid.

There is the 'silence'. But then Bliss walks across the stage, dragging a shovel behind her. No one 'sees' her. It makes a long and otherworldly sound that echoes and echoes.

End of Act One.

Act Two

SCENE ONE

Asquith and Lancelot/Capability Brown meet to discuss progress. Lancelot is somewhat distracted and carries a book.

Lancelot Eleven? Eleven? The plans call for nine hills.

Asquith There was enough ground left over for two more.

Lancelot Stick to the plans. The plans are good ones. If they're followed. Ha. 'Poverty of imagination.' That's what this gutless man wrote (*Reads title.*) *Dissertation on Oriental Gardening*. 'Kitchen-gardeners', he calls us.

Asquith Yes. I've seen it: 'Peasants emerge from the melon ground to take the periwig and turn professor.' No one will take him seriously –

Lancelot (*interrupts*) Imagine –

He casually tears out a page as he reads and lets the leaf fall as he speaks.

– he advocates a return to the grottoes of thirty years ago. How Chambers ever became treasurer of the Royal Academy – (*Tears another.*) And yet I will not honour his vicious attack with a published reply. No. (*Reads.*) 'Whole woods . . . swept away to make room for a little grass and a few American weeds.' (*Tears another.*)

Silence a moment, then:

Lancelot/Asquith Bastard.

Lancelot throws the damaged book to Asquith.

Lancelot The good news is, William Mason is composing a poem defending both my personhood and my work. And even better, Walpole has encouraged Mason to write it. It soothes my heart. Just a bit. (*Beat.*) Back to the practicalities: what's this about the loss of tools? It seems a garden-shed full has been stolen. Other tools broken.

Asquith We've had a lot of rain. Work's stalled. The villagers are sullen. I've got an entire regiment to keep an eye on –

Lancelot (*interrupts*) I won't have them eating my tools. (*Lancelot has a short coughing fit.*)

Asquith I think they're selling them.

Lancelot (*recovering*) That was a little joke. You're not looking well. Lighthouse bothering you again?

Asquith Actually I haven't had that dream in weeks.

Lancelot Good news.

Asquith Because I cannot sleep. I'll be frank. I have a woman on my mind.

Lancelot No.

Asquith From the village.

Lancelot Christ –

Asquith She's not. Common. She can read. She supports the moving of the village –

Lancelot You cannot marry her.

Asquith I don't want to marry her. I just want. I want.

Lancelot It won't prove worth it. And let me tell you, your own hand at night is better than a woman's, if you do it right.

Asquith We have not yet. Been intimate.

Lancelot Good man. Keep it that way.

Asquith I want her. But I'm not even enjoying myself. At night. Truth be told, I can't bear to touch myself.

Lancelot Why's that? Something wrong? Something wrong with. With your. *Pinus rigida*? (*Laughs.*) You don't mind a little joke, do you?

Asquith Please. It's not your concern.

Lancelot (*lowering his voice*) Of course it's my concern. You're my brother. Let's be practical. What. Has it gone. Floppy?

Asquith No. That's not the problem.

Lancelot takes a ruler from his pocket and holds it out between them, and demonstrates.

Lancelot I've learned a 'Capability' trick or two with all my travelling. Look here. This is how it's usually done. Fast. Or slow. But mostly it's done like this. On a straight line.

He slides his hand up and down the ruler, masturbating it, but with no erotic emotion whatsoever, just demonstration. Asquith watches in silence.

But that's where the conundrum lies. First point: deep, sustained pleasure cannot be found on a straight line of motion. Second point: we handle our instrument far too delicately. We treat it like a flower. Bah. You. You have got to be more firm. Brutal even. You've got to – (*Demonstrates.*) – curve it to the left. Curve it to the right. Even if it doesn't like it. Then bend it. Bend it. Until, God damn it, it hurts. It burns. Then shake it, rattle it, as though you mean to throttle it. And then, to finish off, thrust it down, down, between you legs until it's almost uprooted, almost looking right out the back of you. It will feel like it's going to break clean off, but trust me. It won't.

The men stand silently now, gazing at the ruler, which Lancelot slowly lowers now and puts away.

I promise you, you'll sleep like a baby. And you'll stay chaste.

Asquith (*quietly*) Thank you. I'll keep it. In mind.

There is the sound of distant thunder. A gentle storm is coming.

Lancelot You do that. And after you've had a solid night's rest, get on with the work. You're falling behind. Be firm. Don't let them laugh at your back. I'll see you at the end of next month.

SCENE TWO

Jayfort is alone. He sits, and sleeps, as it begins to rain. Then lightning flashes and Bliss appears. Jayfort cannot 'see' her, but we can.

Bliss Hello. Can you see me?

Jayfort Where are you?

Bliss stands in front of him. He addresses her looking in another direction.

Bliss Right in front of you.

Jayfort I can't see you. Am I asleep? Who are you?

Bliss (*sings*)
One little girl
She won't be found,
Seems she flew up
Right out of the ground.

Jayfort A spectre that can rhyme. You're smart then, dangerous.

Bliss Sounds nice when you put it that way. Maybe I am, dangerous. You're not afraid?

Jayfort It's the living I fear. Dead never harmed me.

Bliss You have no hands. I can see all of you but not your hands. Why?

Jayfort Live one day to the next on a ship, quiet, walking low, saying yes, but you get hit. You get hit in the morning. Get hit when the sun's out. Get hit when it's not. You get –

Jayfort/Bliss – hit –

Jayfort – when you're sleeping. When you're laughing. When you're pissing. You get –

Jayfort/Bliss – hit –

Jayfort – when you're not even there. So I learned. My hands are not my own now. Dead hands. They live only to.

Jayfort/Bliss Hit back.

Bliss If you close your eyes again you'll see me.

Jayfort closes his eyes.

Jayfort Yes. I see you now.

Bliss Am I pretty?

Jayfort No. But you are cold and clear. A lake at night.

Bliss How do you remember when you don't know what it is you have forgotten? Tell me.

Jayfort I think there's a map at the back of the head. Problem is we're born with our eyes looking in the other direction.

Bliss I'm not afraid of your hands.

Jayfort holds out a hand. Bliss lightly touches it, then lets go and disappears.

SCENE THREE

Jayfort and Slip lean on their shovels while Castle holds out the two broken pieces of his.

Castle Fuckin' rain. Digging fourteen hours a day, fourteen days a week, and then this morning, found it snapped in half. Soldiers must of done it.

Jayfort You'll pay for it.

Castle throws the pieces aside and begins to get out tobacco.

Slip You can borrow mine.

Slip throws Castle his shovel. Castle involuntarily catches it, dropping his tobacco in the process.

Castle Whoreson.

Jayfort now throws his shovel at Slip, who catches it. A game ensues, the shovels passed between the diggers.

Jayfort You dig, My Lady.

Slip After you, My Lord.

Castle No, please, I insist.

Jayfort I absolutely –

Castle Grigsniputely –

Slip Will desist.

They stop abruptly, each hurriedly going for his shovel, with Slip unhappily retrieving half of the broken one, when Nutley and Scarth enter pulling the tree-moving machine. They are followed by Asquith. Asquith stares at the diggers, especially Slip, who attempts to dig with only the stick of his shovel. Asquith dismisses the soldiers with a nod. They leave, making rude gestures at the diggers.

Asquith You three, over here. (*to Slip*) That will be deducted from your provisions.

The three diggers crowd around the machine. They begin to try and straighten the damage to the machine. Asquith directs them.

Asquith Crushed. It's been crushed. Straighten these bars. And those. This machine is for the small trees. Small as in your height and your height. What imbecile would attempt to move a forty-foot oak with a few bits of wire?

Castle It was the soldiers, sir. They couldn't get the roots loose and they were jumping up and down –

Asquith climbs onto the frame of the tree-mover and begins to pull some small branches loose that are caught in the gears. While he is irritated, he works at being jovial.

Asquith (*interrupts*) Bloody fools. We'll have to have another one built, three times as large. Get back to work, then. Soldiers! 'You cannot guess who I've hired to dig your hills for you,' my brother said: 'Soldiers.' Ha. I've had to show them which end of the shovel you stick in the ground. But never mind. All is well.

Only now do we become aware of Simone elsewhere on stage. Asquith notices her as well. Simone paints, absorbed in her work.

Pardon me. You must be Simone Faulks. Asquith Brown, at your service. Lord Heywood mentioned that you –

Simone (*interrupts*) I have met your brother. He is at Compton Verney, is he not?

Asquith Why, yes. And here, and at Syon House and Alnwick and Radly in Oxfordshire, all at once.

Simone Capability Brown is much sought after.

Asquith We're of the same mind, he and I.

Simone But not of the same fame.

Asquith Fame is a whimsy. Talent's in the eye –

Simone (*interrupts*) Your eye, Mr Brown? Where as a few months ago I was painting green and trees, in a matter of weeks, it's gone to mud.

Asquith picks up some soil and sniffs deeply. Simone winces.

Asquith Ah. English soil. Wonderful stuff. Anything can grow in it. We've brought in three species of pine from the colonies and already they're flourishing. And my favourite, the Northern Pitch Pine. It's a conical conifer. And the cones, a deep red-brown no painter can match but in dreams. The tree is my true mentor, after my dear brother, of course. A tree has no desire. Water and light it requires, little more. It does not whine or fret or sulk. It just lives or dies, without the frills of testament.

He throws the dirt carelessly aside and it hits one of the workmen, who keep on working. Asquith studies her painting.

Asquith May I be permitted?

Simone Since you have already destroyed the view, you might as well dissect mine.

Asquith I am a gentleman.

Simone So you say.

Asquith I think that your view . . . has great merit. But. May I suggest? It's a bit constricted. It requires, considering the recent improvements, a more airy, open feel . . . What's that there?

Simone Flowers.

Asquith There are none out there.

Simone There were, and should be, for flowers signify frailty, the fleeting nature of our lives, Mr Brown.

Castle stops his work. He looks about him, a bit at a loss. The two speakers don't notice him.

Asquith Hmmm. Such obvious fabrications, flowers. Cowslip, tulippa, gilly flower, bah. They cut space into ever smaller pieces. Too . . . insular. By opening up space, by expanding one's prospect, I bring the wild of the world a little closer to home. It is an illusion as well, but a far more satisfying one.

Castle tries out a couple of places but there is no privacy for him to piss.

Simone Your throwing up of hills and filling lakes pretends towards a view that is infinite. But it lacks detail, the way an empty sky does.

Castle finally settles on a place to piss and pisses while Simone and Asquith continue to speak. Then he goes back to work on the machine.

Asquith Miss Faulks. Let me assure you that while my brother and I are cut from the same cloth, we are not exactly of a piece. Like you, at times, such open space leaves me uncertain; with eyes stuck to the horizon, one could go blind. What we are doing here is something that will last for generations. Permanence, leaning forward into time.

Simone You are destroying this landscape!

Asquith No. We are changing it. And that's no easy feat.

Simone Damn you. Damn you.

Asquith Well then, may I assume that you will not be inclined to have a meal with me this evening?

Simone Certainly not. I do not dine with murderers. And you, Mr Asquith, are a variation on the murderer: one day it's green, old England, the next day it's. Muck. Dead muck.

Asquith My dear Miss Falks, the landscape you mourn may have been old, but it was not true. What I'm doing now is no more artificial than the planting of those hedges a hundred years ago, may they rest in peace.

Simone It will take decades for these fields to recover. And this final canvas, this so-called art you have created, will bring us no visual pleasure or reward for neither you nor I will live to see it.

Asquith That is true. But tell me, Miss Faulks, does one create merely for the rewards of visual or tactile pleasure? I do not think so. I think it more likely one creates so that one can sleep at night. And even then, sleep does not often come. Because even the faces of those we will love tomorrow, begin to come apart in our hands today. The simple question is how to make the world stay with us a little while so that we are not alone.

Simone Have you no remorse for what was once here, under your feet?

Asquith slips in what must be Castle's piss, of which he is unaware. Castle now continues to try and straighten the tree-machine as Jayfort and Castle start to drag it away.

Let me show you something, Mr Asquith. (*Simone puts down her paints and speaks to Castle.*) Step closer, you.

Castle is surprised but follows her orders. Jayfort and Slip stop dragging the machine off. They watch. Asquith also watches curiously.

Simone Close your eyes.

Castle Excuse me, ma'am, But I –

Asquith (*interrupts*) Do as you're told.

Castle does so.

Simone This fellow creature, Mr Asquith, is nothing like your landscape, your distant water and hills. He will not last. In a few years, he will be food for beetles. Now, he is a flower. A short full bloom, a burst of colour, and then he dies. He looks robust. So does your landscape. But move a little closer, and there is something else.

Simone, without fuss, pulls open Castle's shirt so that his chest is bare. Then she bends her head and takes hold of one of his nipples with her teeth and sucks at it a moment. Castle is stunned but keeps himself from jumping back.

Asquith Well, yes, I see . . . That.

Castle now fumbles to cover his chest.

That. What has that. To do. With . . . your vision?

Slip (*aside*) She's sucked his nipple!

Simone Up close, right between my teeth, but connected to the greater part that flickers and breathes and boasts with life. An impermanence that *is* infinite. That is what I hope to capture in my vision. (*Beat.*) God's world, before you fiddled with it, Mr Brown, was never *meant* to last.

Simone casually returns to her painting. Asquith seems momentarily at a loss for words. Castle is watching him. They regard one another some moments.

Asquith Get to work.

SCENE FOUR

Scarth and Nutley are laying rolls of sod.

Scarth If you won't bury them, then burn them outside the grounds. Sleeping with them in the tent. Sick man, you are.

Nutley (*removing a small bone from his pocket and gazing at it*) At night they make a humming sound, little snatches of music. (*Nutley hums bits of odd tune.*)

Scarth How many rolls of this we got to lay? Not so bad as digging.

Nutley Can't burn them. Can't bury them. It's not right. Bye bye, my little ones, Adieu. Nope. I'll think of something.

Scarth Trouble, trouble when Mister Brown finds out. You keep them hid.

Nutley They're not happy. I think they like the air.

Scarth You need some air. Ah, I like this rolling grass. Feel like a bit of God myself: and let there be a little grass where there was none. Abracadabra.

Leafeater appears.

Leafeater A man is going to die.

The soldiers are afraid. Leafeater glances over his shoulder.

Tip toe, tip toe, death is coming. On little stick legs.

Scarth Lost two men last night to the fever. Half the regiment is green with it. Maybe you brought the sickness?

Leafeater Pick up your tents and go. In my sleep, I saw a man die.

Scarth Awake, I seen men die. In my lap. What do you want?

Nutley (*sniffs him*) You should wash up. Ugh!

Leafeater In my sleep. I saw.

Scarth You're not a digger.

Leafeater I saw.

Nutley has approached Leafeater. He spits on the corner of his shirt and proceeds to wipe clean a little spot on Leafeater's face. Leafeater doesn't notice.

Leafeater I was swimming and below in the water I saw a dead man floating, his face was soft and when I touched his cheek-

Nutley There. You see? There.

Leafeater – it came apart in my hands.

Nutley Pink as a baby underneath.

Leafeater I saw a dead man. Listen to me. My shoulders are covered with blood. Someone is gnawing through my back to reach my heart.

Nutley Let's have a look, then. Go on.

In exasperation, Leafeater raises his shirt to expose his back to the men. There is no blood or trauma. Nutley inspects him.

Scarth Never been flogged. For sure he's not one of us. Don't touch him. Could be carrying.

Nutley touches Leafeater's back. Leafeater flinches but lets him do so. With his fingers, he slowly traces down the backbone.

Nutley So close below the skin. Your bones. So close but I can't touch them. Almost, almost. (*Beat.*) But not while you live.

Leafeater is somewhat disturbed and looks at Nutley's hand.

Nutley No blood on my hands, see? You're not bleeding.

Suddenly Leafeater grabs Nutley roughly by the collar.

Leafeater You have no idea. Give me your shovel.

Leafeater sees a shovel nearby so he releases Nutley. He picks it up and breaks it across his knee.

Scarth Damn you. We'll pay for that. (*Scarth picks up the broken pieces. He hesitantly pushes Leafeater with the stick end.*) Piss off now.

Leafeater stumbles, then falls on his knees. Scarth is uncertain.

You're upsetting the work. You don't belong here.

Leafeater doesn't move, so Scarth throws the piece aside in disgust. Nutley moves to Leafeater as though to help him up.

No. Leave him be. Trouble enough already. Let's be gone.

Scarth and Nutley begin to exit.

Leafeater Once upon a time . . .

They stop and listen.

I was a. Gentle youth.

Nutley and Scarth leave. Leafeater remains on his knees, alone. Then Bliss appears.

Bliss I heard you walking. You've come back from your travels.

Leafeater (*gets to his feet*) You're not here. Go away.

Bliss I knew you'd come back.

Leafeater Stop following me. You cannot hurt me.

Bliss Hurrump. Hurrah. Hooray.

Leafeater No. No. You're a spoonful of mud I stir in my tea. One swallow and you're gone.

Bliss I hear your throat at night. When you are swimming. Click. Click. Click. For years. That dry. You cannot sleep. Your shit is wet with blood.

Leafeater What do you want?

Bliss For you to tell me what happened. For you to call my name.

Leafeater I can't. Go away.

Bliss Call my name.

Leafeater I don't know it.

Bliss Not the name but what it sounds like. The story inside the name. I can do it. Can you play follow the leader? This is the sound of my name: la, la, la. (*Beat.*) Do it.

Leafeater You're not here.

Bliss I have always been here. Do it. There's no other way. La, la, la.

Leafeater (*silent some moments staring at her, then he copies her sounds*) La, la, la.

Bliss nods, then sings the 'sound' or 'story' of her name. She does not use words, just sounds, beginning with 'la, la, la.' After each sentence of 'music', Leafeater copies her. Then the song turns dark, almost frightening. Leafeater attempts to follow it. Suddenly Bliss makes a noise that is terrible and ugly. It is louder than her small body can make, and echoes all around them. Leafeater does not attempt to copy this sound. Then there is a silence. Bliss waits for him to copy her.

Leafeater (*like the first notes*) La, la, la.

Bliss steps towards him menacingly, and he steps back.

Bliss That's not what happened.

Leafeater Hush, child. It's prettier this way.

SCENE FIVE

The diggers and the villagers are meeting. Only Hesp is not there. As they exchange words, the villagers hold out sacks. Into the sacks Jayfort, Castle and Slip put small trees and turf.

Villager Four/Algren Looks like a weed, mine does. You sure this is from a foreign land?

Castle That sapling is a *Pinus zumdonbriggatapaddawad-wad*. From Africa.

Villager One/Lonoff Green. Green. Crunch to the gristle and chew. Shhh . . .

Villager Two We gave you food last week. What asses do you take us for? These trees are no exchange.

Jayfort In the larger towns, these trees will sell like hot cakes. Just make sure you tell them they're from the colonies.

Villager Four/Algren We need tools. Something we can sell.

Ellen That's right. These trees are worthless. Get us tools.

The diggers continue to hand out the saplings.

Villager Two No. We can't steal from Lord Heywood. He's never stole from us.

Ellen The tools belong to that gardener. It won't hurt our lord.

Slip That's a –

Castle – pudding-porket pine.

Slip And this one's a –

Castle Pifflenoggin' pine. And here, the rarest heg-a-podge-zownut pine. It's cones are like the back of the hedge-hog.

Ellen Give us tools to sell. Anything. Or it's no deal.

After a moment, the diggers look at one another and shrug. Then each take some small tools from their pockets and give them to the villagers.

Villager Two You're still city bastards for taking our jobs.

Villager One/Lonoff Bark, bark. Away. Go home. Jaw-dog.

The two sides just stare at one anther.
Slip distracts the crowd.

Slip (*to Ellen*) Hey, good woman. We've done our deal. Now it's time to celebrate.

Slip holds out his hand. When Ellen won't take it, he claps out a rhythm. The Villagers are distracted a moment and look on with interest. Slip begins to dance. It is a lively dance though it begins rather awkwardly. Suddenly, he slips and falls.

All Villagers Stupid idiot. Pillock. What a clown, etc.

But Jayfort starts clapping the rhythm again, and then Castle. Slip gets up and tries again. What Slip dances is a kind of wild, almost obscene sailors' dance – and though he is not very graceful, he makes up for it with exuberance. Without warning, Jayfort joins in. He dances this sailors' dance as well, though slightly differently. Then Castle joins in too. Now the villagers join in, clapping. For some moments the three men dance together. The villagers are impressed.

Nutley appears with his rifle and fires in the air. The villagers and diggers freeze. Nutley carries a sack. He opens the sack and spills the bones, and the skull, into a pile in front of them. The villagers are afraid.

Nutley Awake, they are. Under my bed. Found them in the fields. The lord said burn them. Master Brown said bury them. But you can't bury a thing that's awake. All night. Can't sleep. In my ear, I hear them say: 'We lived. We lived. Ding. Ding. Ding. But no one knows our name.'

SCENE SIX

Hesp and Asquith together. He is examining the soil.

Hesp You should have come to us when you found the bones.

Asquith I should have. I'm sorry. It was Lord Heywood's wish there be no stir.

Hesp Lord Heywood has a reputation for honesty.

Asquith Look. It's common to find bones when you dig.

Hesp Not on this land. No wrong was ever done on this estate. The village is upset. And frightened.

Asquith (*only now facing her, with a slight threat*) Then tell them the matter is being taken care of. Nothing to worry about. Do you understand?

Hesp Your brother may have the ear of the King but it is you who are digging in the mud. You should be careful not to offend any more than you have.

Asquith (*taken aback, but amused*) Well, well. I regret having offended you at all. Lord Heywood has already ordered that the remains be brought to the churchyard for a proper burial. But I don't like threats. Especially from you . . .

Hesp Trouble is not what I want.

Asquith Well, trouble is what you are, for I have been watching the fields all week, in the hopes of seeing you out there. Will she come today? I ask myself a hundred times.

Hesp And a hundred times I tell myself: do not go there again. He is tired of your face.

Asquith I am tired only of waiting for you to come and speak with me. (*Beat.*) Come. There is something I want to show you. Cover your eyes.

Hesp covers her eyes. Asquith leads her to a spot where she can 'view' the fields below.

Now look. *Voilà.*

Hesp gasps. She is awed.

Where once there was nothing but land as flat and ugly as a tin plate, you have – (*He sweeps with his arm.*) – this.

Hesp claps her hands excitedly.

Asquith And not two or three but seven new green hills. As though –

Hesp As though they had sprung up from the earth on their own accord.

Asquith (*pleasantly surprised*) Exactly.

Hesp Then you are almost done.

Asquith Almost. Not quite. I want you. To understand me. What I am doing here. This work. I want you to (*Beat.*) speak to your friends in the village. Encourage them to move.

Hesp I have already done so. I want the selling of our leases. And almost half of us, we're happy to move. I think it's a good plan.

Asquith For that I am grateful.

He attempts to embrace her but she backs away.

Hesp Mr Asquith. Please. I. I.

Asquith What is it you want then? I don't understand you. Tell me.

Hesp I want you –

Asquith Yes.

Hesp I want you –

Asquith And I want you.

Hesp – to open your pants.

Asquith (*unsettled*) What?

Hesp I want to look at you.

Asquith Such a. Request. Does not become a lady.

Hesp I'm not a lady.

Asquith But I am a gentleman.

Hesp Do it, please, or I will go and not come here again.

Asquith Do you wish me to lose my mind?

Hesp says nothing but waits. Asquith looks about him to make sure they're alone. Asquith, his back to the public, takes his penis out of his pants. Hesp looks. Asquith waits.

Hesp You are not different to any man.

Asquith No.

Hesp I'm glad then.

Asquith And for such an act of debasement, what shall I receive in return?

Hesp The pleasure of me watching you. Go on. Touch yourself. Please. Yes. Look at me. Look at my face. Can you not see how I want to touch you?

Asquith masturbates as she watches.

I can hear you breathe now, even from this distance. Yes. As though you were about to choke. As though you –

Asquith suddenly stops.

Hesp Why do you stop? Don't stop. Don't stop now. Please.

Asquith closes his pants.

Asquith This is. This is. Not right. I feel like a. Whore.

Hesp Mr Brown. When you laugh . . . When you laugh I hear treasure spill from the hands of great men. When you speak, regiments of horses turn. Close your eyes and my world goes dark.

Asquith Such powers I've never had. And never will.

Hesp Can you love me as you would love a lady?

Asquith I do not know. I could try.

She takes his hand. She pushes it against the dress cloth over her crotch.

Hesp Here. Touch my frock. Just to look at you, I am wet even on the outside.

Asquith touches the wetness, then puts his hand deep into the material. Hesp takes in a deep breath and holds it.

SCENE SEVEN

Nutley, Scarth, Slip, Jayfort, and Castle sit together, taking a rest from digging. Jayfort has removed his boots and is rubbing his feet. The others watch him. They begin to follow suit.

Jayfort Just a common poacher. A thief. Like us. And we're not evil, so it makes you look again at what's –

Slip I'm not like Satan, thank you kindly.

Jayfort Look at it another way.

Scarth Satan is Satan.

Castle Can't argue with that.

Jayfort Picture it. Close your eyes. All of you.

They do so. He checks.

There's this garden, a paradise, surrounded by defences – walls, gigantic trees, a

steep wilderness, whose hairy sides
With thicket overgrown, grotesque and wild –

Scarth Fair description of your feet there, Slip.

Jayfort – a steep and savage hill guarded by

strict sentries and stations thick
Of angels watching round.

Sound familiar?

Slip No.

They all open their eyes, look around, and shake their heads.

Scarth Not a lot of angels in my life, good or bad.

Castle Look, you're rowing against the current, no matter what Mr John Mildown says.

Jayfort Mil-ton. And he doesn't say it. I'm saying it.

Scarth What?

Slip You can't just go and say something different. You didn't write it. Have some respect. Oh, my poor feet.

Jayfort Listen. Here's this outlaw –

Nutley Satan.

Jayfort Right. And he's an outcast who's trying to get into this . . . this royal park because the king or lord has put him in a gaol for rebelling. He escapes and goes after the king's prize deer.

Nutley Adam and Eve.

Jayfort But he's picked up by the king's patrol. The point is, maybe the lowest and the worst of us –

Nutley That's you lot.

Jayfort Maybe they got a right to steal and poach and've only been seen as out*laws* since they don't get to write the *laws*. The point is –

Castle The point is, whatever kind of theives we are, we keep selling the tools, we'll have nothing to work with and soon be digging with our hands.

Slip Oh, look at my feet.

They all look at Slip's feet.

Jayfort No, the point is . . . (*to Slip*) God, man, what a mess!

Slip Blood blisters, skin rot, and my toes are turning yellow.

Nutley The bones are safe though.

Scarth Will you shut up about bones, you cannibal. (*to Jayfort*) No offence.

Jayfort Fungus.

Scarth What, me?

Jayfort That's yellow toe. Means he's got fungus under his toenails.

Slip That's what it is? Smells bad when you squeeze it out. Have a look.

The others all lean in to watch the operation. Villager Three walks past carrying an exotic plant. He joins the others. All the men, except for the villager, have their shoes off and are airing their feet..

Villager Three I like toes myself. If you suck on them, it makes the hair grow from grey to black. Young again. But yours don't look pretty.

Castle Yellow toe.

Slip Thank you.

Jayfort The larger question is, do you tell your woman right out or do you just pray it never comes to her attention?

Castle Depends what her feet are like. I mean if she's got sheets of skin peeling away in slivers that smell of pike, perch, and dimplewhipper fish then, well, you've got nothing to hide.

Villager Three Least you've got a full house. Two of mine turned black overnight. Pulled them off in the morning. (*Sings.*) One, two, and it's off to work I go.

Nutley And the bones?

Villager Three Just disappeared. Ssssssshhh.

There is a moment of silence.

Scarth Went back to the hole where we found the bones. Something else there too. Found a rope.

Jayfort What kind of rope?

Scarth takes out a piece of rope.

Scarth The good kind. Strong braid. Well tied.

Villager Two What are you saying?

Nutley The kind that fits around the neck.

SCENE EIGHT

Leafeater, alone, talking to himself. As he speaks he'll take a few leaves from his pocket and absentmindedly smell them.

Leafeater Gamekeeper. Ash, Ash Pidduck, that was my name. I had fine shoes. Not as fine as my brothers. Be still. Be still, he said. I was the second born. My mother was a horse. That is what my brother told me when he inherited the estate. Lord Heywood. So I became the gamekeeper. I didn't mind. I liked roaming the forest. Running with the deer. Watching their backs. Like angels, the deer were. Hardly touched the ground. My brother said I mustn't let them die. (*Hears something.*) What's that? (*Beat.*) But then the killers came. Not from the village, they were. Village never touched the deer. It was outsiders. That winter, thieves felled half the deer in my brother's forests. Even the deer were near starving. People roamed the land, their bellies full of leaves. They died in heaps by the roadside, covered in snow. But that didn't make it right. To kill my deer. Teach them a lesson, my brother said. And so I did.

One night I caught a poacher in the North Forest. Hardly a man, what was left of him. Birds for eyes, that scared. Be still, be still, I told him. He cried so hard his tooth fell out. It broke my brother's heart to know this thief was no outsider, but a villager he'd trusted. So I told my men what my brother told me: 'Hang him.'

And so we did. Hush, hush. No one would know. Saved the lives of maybe five deer that season. One man for five deer.

Years later. Now. They couldn't move that same tree. Broke the machine. I was the gamekeeper. Hurrump, hurrah, hooray. Shhhh. Only it wasn't in the month of May. It was the month of dance, dance, and blue flesh and cold. (*Beat.*) I couldn't walk out of that season.

SCENE NINE

Slip seems to be reading, casually, a book. Only he is reading his hands, as though he were holding a book open in them. Villager One/Lonoff appears. They study one another. Slip goes on reading and Villager One is curious.

Villager One/Lonoff Cities? Your fingers? (*Beat.*) Cities? Men lie dead in a juggler's sun.

Slip Get away. Idiot. Pig ate half your brain when you were born. That's what your brethren say.

Villager One/Lonoff Rocks, stones, won't move. Worms sing content. Won't move.

Slip So you're one of them that don't want to move? Slowing up our work, you are. Lord Heywood's too soft on the lot of you. I say pull your houses down. That'll make you run for a new roof.

Villager One now copies Slip. Begins to read, confidently, only he is reading the back on his hands.

Slip You can't read like that. You got your book upside down. (*Slip adjusts Villager One's hands.*) And when you're done with that page, you turn to the next page, like this.

Slip folds his hands together, opens them again, as though a page has been turned. Villager One catches on and does the same. Now they both read. Suddenly Villager One gets very intent on what he is reading: he giggles, he grunts, he scoffs. Slip gets distracted and comes to see what Villager One is reading. Villager One pulls away and hides his 'pages'.

Bastard. Why can't I see? I taught you to read.

Villager One backs away further.

You read it to me then.

Villager One/Lonoff Cities. In shells. Killing frost that cast to February. Penguins shrunk and friar. Nine times his baleful eyes furnace the song. Pure shepherd of sea. Oh, transatlantic . . .

Slip Transatlantic? That's a big word to read. Go on.

Villager One/Lonoff Transatlantic . . . lasting pain. Treat or bitter the dirty kiss. Mercy, mercy as the snow and ice of trickery. Gibber. Gibber. Gibber. In the end.

Slip Hmmm. You're an idiot. What do you think it means?

Villager One/Lonoff It's all loud nonsense and sad, crude intent. But words lining up, out of order, bring cold, sweet hope to my heart and illuminate the dark. And it is getting darker, slowly, slowly, do you not agree?

Slip So you can talk sense?

Villager One/Lonoff No. I leave that to the rest of you. (*Villager One closes his 'book'.*)

SCENE TEN

Asquith and Hesp are alone in the fields together.

Asquith Please. You must go. Go home. There's much to be done. When I see you, I can't help myself. You mustn't come here every day.

Hesp Oh. (*Beat.*) You told me to come.

Asquith And you have come, my sweet. Again and again in these days. More times than I have, I may add.

Hesp You are a good lover, sir.

Asquith I only wish it did not always have to be. Here. On the ground. It seems, somehow, predictable. 'And just where do you do these fumblings?' My brother would say. 'In the mud,' I would have to answer. 'Predictable,' he would say. And he would be right.

Hesp Is that wrong? We have nowhere else to –

Asquith (*interrupts*) It certainly is no surprise. I think if Lord Heywood came upon us, wheezing and grunting, he would not be surprised. A gentleman twitching with a lovely maid below him is not an all too uncommon sight.

Hesp Grunting. Twitching. I thought our love-making more. Delicate, sir.

Asquith (*playing*) Delicate? You? My darling, have you heard yourself? When you come you sound like a crowd of drunken priests cursing Our Lord for the advent of wine.

Hesp Please, sir. Do not laugh at me.

Asquith Oh, come here, my darling. Do not pout.

Hesp But there's work to do, sir. So you say.

Asquith We can be quick. There's no one about.

Asquith embraces her but Hesp pulls away.

And this sort of teasing is also predictable. It does not become you, Hesp. (*Asquith tries to take her arm.*)

Hesp Stop it. Please. You know I want to win your heart. Tell me how. There is nothing I would not do.

Asquith Well then, surprise me. Surprise me!

Hesp I thought that I had done so in giving myself to you.

Asquith That was no real surprise, however delightful. Hesp. Oh, Hesp. Can you not. Make me. Blind. As I have turned this earth, can you not turn me. (*Beat.*) I have woken this landscape, wake me up!

Hesp I do not know how.

Asquith Then that is your failure, sweet one, not mine. Really, you must go. I have work to do.

Hesp Sir. Do you still want me? Now?

Asquith Yes, but I –

Hesp (*interrupts*) Then give me your word that you will do what I ask, at this moment. And I will surprise you.

Asquith Just what are you up to –

Hesp (*interrupts*) Give me your word or you will never know.

Asquith All right then. I give you my word.

Hesp Good. Now. Stay where you are, but your trousers to your knees, sir.

Asquith Silly girl.

Glancing about but following her orders, he drops his pants. His long shirt covers him so we do not see his nakedness.

(*Sighs.*) I know what you're up to now. You're going to relieve me with your mouth –

Hesp (*interrupts*) Do not speak, sir.

Asquith (*enjoying this*) Yes, ma'am.

Hesp Look. (*Hesp reaches under her skirt and touches herself, briefly, practically. Then she holds up her hand.*) My whole hand is wet. From wanting you already.

Asquith Let me touch you now.

Hesp No. Get on your knees.

A little unsure, but Asquith does it.

Now close your eyes.

Asquith starts to protest but Hesp shushes him.

You gave your word, as a gentleman.

Asquith shuts up. Hesp pushes him over so he is now on his hands and knees with Hesp behind him. Hesp puts her hand on his back and slowly traces his backbone. Then her hand disappears under his shirt and after a moment Asquith gasps.

Asquith Stop that. You can't –

Hesp Be quiet, sir. (*Hesp continues.*)

Asquith But that's. Impossible –

Hesp Shut up, sir. You gave your word. As a gentleman.

Asquith (*weakly*) Please don't. It. Hurts.

Hesp Then don't resist me. Relax, sir. Yes, relax.

Asquith (*uncomfortable*) You can't go any further.

Hesp Keep breathing. It's all right. I promise.

Asquith groans, both with pain and pleasure.

Asquith Sweet Christ –

Hesp I have a small hand.

Asquith – in Heaven.

Hesp And I'm missing my thumb, remember?

Asquith (*speaks haltingly*) This. Is. Not. A.

Hesp Just a little further.

Asquith Gen. Tle. Man. Ly.

Hesp Almost there.

Asquith Thing. To. Do. (*Asquith cries out, once, then is still.*)

Hesp There. Shhh. It's all right. We're in.

Asquith is stunned, almost delirious with the pain and pleasure.

Do I surprise you now, Mr Brown? Are you awake? (*Hesp now moves her hand back and forth inside him.*)

Asquith Oh. (*Beat.*) My. (*Beat.*) God.

Hesp curls down over him.

SCENE ELEVEN

Ellen is writing another letter. This time she is alone and simply speaks her letter.

Ellen My dearest . . . husband. I am sending this letter to Pennsyl. Vannia. It is not on the coast, like the others, and I know you like the waters, but perhaps by now you have drifted inland. (*Beat.*) There is something I must tell you: I can no longer remember your face. But last night I dreamt about you, and in the dream your face was as clear and familiar to me as my own. You were wearing your old blue shirt. As I tied it for you, your breath passed across my cheek and left a shadow. (*Beat.*) The crops are weak this season. But good news: we shall share a goat with old Mrs Robinson. There is something dark in the air when I wake these mornings. I don't know what it is. At first light I lie awake and listen to Hesp breathe beside me. It is an effort to get out of bed. When I stand at the door and look at the new day coming, something moves behind me, but when I turn, it is gone. Perhaps one day I shall turn around and it will be staring me in the face. Will there be a name for it on this earth? And if it has a name, will I find a way to speak it?

SCENE TWELVE

Simone is arranging a still life of sticks and twigs, which make a kind of 'bed'. Hesp watches her. Simone rearranges the 'mattress'. Hesp is silent. Finally Simone is ready for Hesp.

Simone Come now. While the light is still strong.

She motions to Hesp to get in the still life. Hesp hesitates.

Simone Did you not come to pose in my portrait?

Hesp No. I'm sorry, ma'am.

Simone Well. That damn Heywood said he'd send a woman to pose as a maid. Would you mind, then? I will give you some cake for your troubles.

Hesp goes where Simone leads her.

Now lie down and pretend to sleep, curled up on those sticks. Oblivious to the world around you. Dreaming of sheep or milk cows and the like. That's right. Don't move.

Hesp lies down awkwardly. Simone sketches. Hesp moves slightly.

Don't move. Relax.

Hesp It pricks.

Simone Sleep. That's it. Sleep. (*Simone sketches.*)

Hesp Is this your work?

Simone It is a labour. Yes. But of love.

Hesp I do not love my labour.

Simone No. But what of that pompous Mr Asquith?

Hesp (*rising. Simone motions for her to lie back. She does*) What do you mean, ma'am?

Simone I have eyes. Ears. And many other unappreciated facilities, I might add.

Silence reigns while Simone sketches.

Hesp He is pompous, isn't he, ma'am?

They giggle together.

Simone And he has a habit when he laughs of –

Hesp Snorting.

They laugh together, delighting in a secret companionship.

Simone Yes. (*Pause.*) But you must realise that he will not take you away. Well, a mile or two perhaps, then –

Hesp Drop me like a hot coal?

Simone stops sketching. She considers Hesp.

Simone This is no good. Come away from there. Damn this . . . work. I cannot paint when my subject has disappeared.

Hesp looks at Simone's sketch.

Hesp Can you not paint what it used to look like, out there?

Simone It is difficult to remember.

She stands with Hesp and directs Hesp's gaze. She puts her arm comfortingly around Hesp's shoulder.

What do you see when you look at this landscape? I see nothing. I am no longer out there, you see. There is nothing in this new landscape that remembers me. And it's me that I want to be remembered. Me. But everything is dissolving before my eyes. If I stay here, I think they will mistake me for a tree grown up in the wrong place, snatch me up with that terrible machine of theirs and plant me elsewhere, very deep, and then it will be too late to move on. You, you want to leave. All I've wanted was to be something more than Lord Heywood's not extremely talented cousin painter. And yet I think it must take perhaps a very special talent to recognise that one has simply failed. I shall have to think seriously of marriage. What a bind. I'm going home to Dorset.

Hesp continues to look at the landscape. There is the sound of a 'smack.' Hesp takes a small step backwards and looks questioningly at Simone. Again we hear the smack of what sounds at first like a hammering. It's a sound we know but cannot quite place. It slowly grows louder.

SCENE THIRTEEN

Slip is standing with his hands tied behind his back. Castle is methodically slapping him in the face, but hard, brutally. Asquith stands turned away from this spectacle. Jayfort stands quietly elsewhere.

Asquith That's enough. (*Asquith now moves close to question Slip.*) My brother will return in a fortnight. I know that you know. Who burned down the shed? Must I hit you myself? (*Suddenly turns on Castle, and Jayfort.*) Perhaps we should tie you up now? Or you?

Jayfort It weren't us, sir.

Asquith But you know who it was.

Castle No, sir.

Asquith You're lying. Oh, dear God explain to me why I was given these kind of men to dig?

Slip Because you're a lucky man, sir.

Asquith What?

Slip To have lived this long. Without our love.

Asquith Are you threatening me?

Slip whistles a few notes like a bird.

Shut up.

Castle I hate birds. He's just doing that to get at me.

Asquith Shut him up.

Slip whistles on quietly.

Castle He's just. Upset, sir. Me being his best friend and all. He's angry 'cause I hit him.

Slip stares hard at Castle.

Slip Nonsense. I love you.

Asquith Best friends? Ha. The notions you people have. What kind of a man would beat his best friend?

Castle You'd have him beat anyway, sir. I'd rather it's myself that does it, than another man.

Asquith Get out of my sight. (*to Jayfort*) You? Are you his friend too?

Jayfort I hate the man, sir.

Asquith Good. Then take that man's place.

Jayfort does so. He looks at Asquith for guidance.

Not in the face this time. In the gut.

Jayfort Yes, sir.

Slip begins his bird sounds again. Jayfort hesitates some moments, but then punches Slip in the gut. Slip does not fall.

Asquith Again. And with a bit more effort.

Jayfort does so, harder. Slip tries to keep making bird sounds but with the punches the sound is slowly knocked out of him. Jayfort also begins to do his 'footwork'. Now the movements come together and he is boxing.

Keep going. Don't stop until I tell you to stop.

Slip finally falls. Jayfort stands over the seemingly unconscious Slip.

Jayfort Brother of mine.

SCENE FOURTEEN

The villagers are in the midst of a discussion. Only Ellen is silent and removed from the others. Villager One sits off to the side, making strange whimpering noises that float in and out of the discussion.

Villager Three Be beaten, and we were beaten.

Villager Two No. Not on this land. He's a good lord. All these years.

Villager Four/Algren (*to Hesp*) It's your Asquith who's ordered the beatings.

Hesp It's Lord Heywood.

Villager Two We have a bond with Lord Heywood. Let's stick to it.

Villager Three Starve, and we starved.

Villager Two But some of us lived!

Villager Three (*to Hesp*) Eyes in your ass, woman.

Villager Four/Algren Others've been beaten. I wrote down their names.

Villager Three Peter Carey's been taken away for burning the sheds. He didn't do it.

Villager Two Wanted to. Never had the chance, poor bastard.

Villager Three A stupid crime, whoever burnt it down. We can't stop the digging.

Hesp The diggers say there's a boat leaves in a fortnight from Liverpool to the colonies. We could go, mother. We could join Father and Bliss. It's not safe here any more.

Villager Three You don't want to join your father.

Hesp Why not?

Villager Four/Algren Gibber for the gallows.

Villager One begins to say 'gibber' over and over. Some others join in.

Ellen Shut up. All of you.

They are all silent.

Villager Four/Algren You know it has to be him. No news from the colonies.

Hesp The bones? Are you talking about the bones?

Villager Two (*to Villager Four*) And what of the girl? What happened to the daughter?

Villager Four/Algren Ellen, it's clear to us, and you.

Hesp What are you saying?

Villager Three What was left of the man they found, it was your father.

Hesp No. My father crossed the ocean. He –

Villager Four/Algren (*interrupts*) He went out hunting at dark, almost sixteen years ago, to get food, to feed you and your sister. And for the rest of us. He never came back. I remember that night.

Hesp No. No one hunted from this village because Lord Heywood was good to us.

Villager Two Lord Heywood kept us alive . . . Just barely. A handful of grain in winter.

Villager Three In return we didn't hunt his deer.

Villager Four/Algren Your father hunted. The night he disappeared Lord Heywood's servants said they seen some men and a child leave in a wagon for Liverpool.

Villager Two Stunk like a rumour. But it's what we wanted to believe.

Villager Four/Algren (*to Ellen*) Your husband. Ha. Not to the colonies. But hanged for poaching. And all those letters, year after year . . .

Villager Three But what happened to the child? (*to Ellen*) You had a small child –

Villager Four/Algren There were lots of small bones too. Must have been the daughter as well.

Hesp (*interrupts, to Ellen*) Lord Heywood killed Father?

Villager Two Not with his own hands.

Hesp But what of my sister? They found only one man's skull!

Villager Four/Algren Sometimes, death leaves no skull behind.

Hesp No. You're all just scared. No.

Villager Three Believe what you like. Bones can't talk.

They are all silent some moments.

Villager Four/Algren (*to Ellen*) I say we'll give up the damn leases when Lord Heywood does the oak jig, just like your husband.

Villager Three That's right. We can't budge now. Let's hold fast.

All Villagers Yeah. / That's right, damn them. / We won't move now. / To hell with Heywood. / Hold fast.

Hesp Is that all you can think about? Holding fast? Winning your battle over a dirty piece of ground? My father was your friend. He was our family. (*to villagers*) Where is your grief? (*to Ellen*) And you, a child and a husband lost. Where is your grief? Not a sound you've made with that big mouth of yours.

Everyone is silent.

Hesp (*to Ellen*) Where is your grief?

Villager Three Grief? Ha. What can that do for us now? We wipe our ass with it.

Suddenly Ellen lets out a terrible scream of pain, but she slaps her own mouth shut with her hands, trying to keep the scream inside her. Only when she has physically subdued her grief does she speak. The villagers are quiet. Ellen now approaches her daughter. She gently strokes her daughters face.

Ellen Go find your Asquith. Tell him we've made our decision: we will not move.

SCENE FIFTEEN

Leafeater is digging a hole with his hands. He is distracted. Bliss appears dragging a shovel for him.

Bliss I knew the names of birds from a book my father had. I was a quick child. My feet were fat with running. Close my eyes, close my eyes and turn, turn in a field that spread out from my arms into seven different countries in my mind. Soup was good. Morning was better. I stuffed my father's coat with leaves and he laughed and laughed. Dance, dance with wooden spoons and a chicken with one leg I named Godiva. (*She stops and faces Leafeater.*) I was. I was. You bastard, I was.

Leafeater Alive.

Bliss Yes. I was alive.

Leafeater I didn't know he was your father. A man was stealing from Lord Heywood –

Bliss (*interrupts*) That's not what I want to know. That's not why I came back. Laugh. Laugh if you like. I can't. I can't . . . I can't remember how I died.

Leafeater (*incredulous*) You can't remember?

Bliss I only remember. The days before that. The snow. Buckets of water. The snail on my finger. My father's big ears.

Leafeater All these years coming after me, haunting me? Gnawing, gnawing at my back and all because your memory failed you? How can this be? You stupid . . . Stupid pitiful . . . if you weren't dead already I'd kill you.

Bliss Tell me or it will never stop.

Leafeater She can't remember how she died! Ha!

Bliss Tell me and I will leave you alone.

Leafeater But I could lie to you, you know? I could say you ran out of the woods when you saw your father hanging and that you fainted, oh my, and fell down dead. Or perhaps you ate a poisoned berry.

Bliss Not berries.

Leafeater shakes his head and laughs. He snatches the shovel from her and begins to dig.

Tell me how I died.

Leafeater I can't. I haven't time. Someone needs a grave.

He continues to dig. Suddenly Bliss attacks him and attempts to wrest the shovel from him. They fight over it.

Let go of it. Let go.

Bliss bites his hand. He cries out. He shoves her and she falls. He raises the shovel to hit her. He freezes.

Bliss Is that what you did?

Leafeater Little bitch. You bit me. There's blood. See? There's blood!

Bliss What did you do?

Leafeater brings the shovel down gently next to Bliss.

Leafeater (*quietly, calmly*) I hit you.

Bliss Once?

Leafeater You kept getting up. You kept running at me.

Bliss (*quietly*) You killed my father.

Leafeater Not with my own hands.

Bliss You said to your men, 'Hang him.' I heard you. I followed my father that night. I used to follow him when he went out hunting. I liked the dark.

Leafeater Be still.

Bliss moves slowly away from Leafeater and remembers, but without reliving the event. Instead, with a calm stillness.

Bliss I came out of the woods and I saw a man hanging. One of my father's boots had slipped off. I could see his toes. He had long toes. Like string beans. I used to tease him –

Leafeater Shut up.

Bliss Father, you have beans for toes.

Leafeater Shut up, girl!

Bliss Beans for toes.

Leafeater swings the shovel and hits a child we cannot see.

Leafeater I said be still. (*He continues methodically to beat at the earth, with great force, with his shovel.*) Be still. (*Swings.*) Be still. (*Swings.*) Be still.

The whacks echo from another time and build to a deafening noise. Bliss stands very still listening to the blows that she received upon her death. Worn out, Leafeater drops the shovel and kneels before the piece of ground he has been bludgeoning. He takes something from his pocket and holds it tight in his hands. He speaks to the object in his hands.

Forgive me, little one. Please. Please. Forgive me.

Bliss What have you got there?

Leafeater slowly brings it from hiding. Bliss stares at it a moment.

Leafeater It's your skull.

Bliss takes it from him, looks the skull in the face.

Bliss Hello. I've been looking for you. Do you remember me?

SCENE SIXTEEN

Slip, Castle, Jayfort and Nutley sit close around a lifeless body: it is Scarth.

Nutley (*to Slip*) Thought it'd be you that would die. All crumpled up on the ground like that, Jayfort hitting you, thump, thump, thump.

Slip Nah, Jayfort was pulling his punches. Most of them, at least. Bastard saved my life.

Slip pulls a couple punches on Jayfort to demonstrate. They laugh, then go suddenly quiet.

Nutley Yesterday he asked me to call him Scarthability. He had big. Plans. Then a red beetle landed on the end of his shovel. Made him laugh. Then he coughed twice and fell down dead. That quick the fever took him. Feel how cold he is now.

Only Nutley touches his friend's cold skin.

Castle He don't know it. Better off. He's gone to the land of Lumberwishken. That's the heaven for our kind. Food enough to eat. Soft bedding.

Slip And if you still can't read by the time you get there, books you can hold, armloads for carrying.

Castle That's right. And clean water. And you can make up any word you like and an angel carves it in stone and keeps it safe. Lumberwishken: the poor man's place of rest.

Nutley No. No. Who would want to die? (*Nutley takes in a few short breaths through his teeth.*) The air. It makes your teeth cold. Alive. Alive. That's what we are. I don't want to die.

Jayfort Three of us are going back to London. You can come with us, you want.

Nutley I'd be shot.

Jayfort We've got places to hide in the City. We'll lay low, then find some work.

Castle Yeah. We could try the docks again first. We could teach you how to build a ship.

Castle and Slip build the following possibility together.

Slip That's right. That only sails in one simple direction: straight fucking ahead!

Castle And the likes of us, one dark night, once it's built, we'll steal that ship from the docks –

Slip – and set sail to some long green island where the tallest trees –

Nutley (*interrupts*) Scarth was my friend. I could cut him now. I could touch his bones and he wouldn't feel it. Always too late. (*Nutley takes out a knife. He rolls back his sleeve.*) Look. (*Nutley makes a small cut in his arm, but deep. He thrusts his arm at the men.*) Touch me. It's deep enough. You can touch the bone. While I'm still alive. Touch me. One of you. Please. Touch me.

The men don't want to touch him. Then Castle comes forward, but Nutley turns away and grabs the collar of the dead man and lifts him a little. He speaks to the dead man.

Who would want to die? (*Beat.*) Not you. Not you. Nor I.

SCENE SEVENTEEN

Asquith is surveying his almost finished landscape. Hesp stands behind him, watching him. Then Asquith realises she is there.

Asquith What a morning. Ha. The entire village came out to confront me. Dozens of them. Stamping and sweating like cattle. Nothing surprising. (*Beat.*) But that you were a part of it.

Hesp steps by him and surveys the land.

Hesp See the smoke from the chimneys. Someone cooks now. Another boiling rags.

Asquith You asked me once if I could love you. I thought perhaps I could. But you were a part of this. You turned against me. You betrayed me. Why?

Hesp Stripped down. With your mouth at my breast, anything I would give away at that moment. To stay with you. (*Beat.*) But afterwards, I walk back to the village. My shoes are always wet. I've never been so cold. Nothing has changed.

Asquith Fucking a gentleman will not always change your life. I could have told you that. As I can tell you that you and the rest of the village will move.

Hesp When you told us to go home. And we began to shout. I'd never raised my voice to a superior. It was like –

Asquith This is not in your hands.

Hesp – splitting open a rock to get at the sound. And all around me people shouting, and something like water rushing in through my head and circling my skull. All of us. Sweating and stamping. Yes. Sweating and shining. You are right. But not like cattle. But as lanterns. Lit up. Lanterns lit up in black water.

Asquith My, my. That bright were you? It changes nothing. You lose.

Hesp It's not about winning.

Asquith It should be.

Hesp No. This is about this moment. Days, years ahead of us might hear what we say now, if we're loud enough. If we –

Asquith (*interrupts*) Posterity doesn't give a damn for your noise. In ten years time you'll be an old woman, Hesp. There won't be another gentleman to make you come in the grass. To carry you away. Twelve more years and you'll be dead. What will you leave behind? Nothing. I will leave behind another kind of England, under which will lie your grave. If you cannot leave a mark, get out of the way of those who can.

For a long moment Hesp is silent. When she speaks again she is calm. She surveys the land around her.

Hesp You have turned this land inside out, but nothing has disturbed the surface. Men with small hearts still rule with rope and guns while we share grass in our bowls and wait for a message, a knock at the door. And when we should stand we lie down on the earth so your shoes will stay dry as you cross this sad world. (*Beat.*) Mr Brown, I had the pride to believe I might change you. But I was wrong. You believe God is your mentor because you perfect his landscape. What an arrogance you have. God laughs at you, Mr Asquith. You are merely a child playing in the mud. Not a tree you have planted, not a hill raised by your own hand. (*Beat.*) You did not create this miracle, other men did.

Asquith You have turned against me. Get out of my sight.

Hesp I have never been in your sight, sir. Until now. You have a sweet mouth. You taste of biscuits. I gasp at the thought of you.

Asquith Come here. Let me touch you again. This work has not been easy.

Hesp You are asleep, Mr Brown. It is different now.

She moves to leave. His voice stops her.

Asquith When you were. Inside me. In those moments, staring at my own hands in the grass. (*Speaks in a continuous stream.*) Terror and pleasure the land around me going out like a light I could have torn the field beneath us wide open such was the power I thought I'd split in two. (*Beat.*) No. I yearned for it. That I would never be again who I was. But I couldn't. I was. Afraid. Afterwards I walked back to the manor without you. The land below my feet came back to steady me and I welcomed that old ground. (*Beat.*) My life did not change. No. That's a lie. I did not let it.

Hesp again moves to go.

Asquith Wait. (*Beat.*) Hesp. Hesp Turner. Do not go. You are everything I. (*Beat.*) Never dreamed.

It takes considerable effort for Asquith to say this.

Stay with me.

Hesp is quiet. She turns and takes a step towards him.

Hesp No. To you I say: no.

They regard one another.

Close your eyes, my love. Day is coming.

Hesp exits. Asquith stands alone. Then we hear the sudden and deafening sound of rushing, crashing water, of water breaking through a barrier and hurling itself forwards.

SCENE EIGHTEEN

It is early morning. Still dim light. Leafeater stands regarding the ruined, flooded landscape. When Leafeater moves aside we see that Bliss has been standing directly behind him, almost as though she were a part of him. Now they separate.

Bliss The worms drown in their beds. The crickets are silent. Nothing more to listen to. I am going back now. To my grave. (*Bliss surveys the landscape.*) You did this. It was you.

Leafeater The fields are under water. No more secrets can be unearthed. The hills have washed away. Yes. I opened the sluice. I released the river. Hirrumph, hurrah, hooray. This cursed landscape is a pig's bath.

Bliss The village still stands.

Leafeater High and dry. Just out of reach of the water. I don't give a damn, but Lord Heywood will appreciate the irony.

Now in the weak light we see the bent and broken frame of a tree-moving machine. It is larger than the one we saw earlier. It is a huge, beautiful sculpture, made the more so by it's destruction. A lifeless form is caught on the machine. It seems almost a part of the ruined sculpture.

Bliss But someone drowned.

Leafeater Yes. A man was trapped inside the tree-moving machine when the river flooded over the fields. I saw it happen. He did not cry out. It was an accident. It could not be helped.

Bliss Touch him.

Leafeater I will not.

Bliss You killed him. You must touch him.

Leafeater looks at her curiously, then he moves to the machine. He tentatively reaches out and touches the dead man's arm.

Leafeater He is cold. His hair is thick with mud.

Bliss Do you remember?

Leafeater I remember everything.

Bliss No. (*Beat.*) Do you remember?

Leafeater is silent. He touches the man's hair, tenderly. He looks at Bliss.

Tell me then.

Leafeater is still, then he pulls the man's head back to see his face. He steps back, his eyes on the dead man's face.

Leafeater (*horror*) This. This man. (*Beat.*) This dead man –

Bliss – is you.

Leafeater Yes. This dead man. Is me.

Bliss and Leafeater stare at one another in silence. He realises that he is dead.

SCENE NINETEEN

Lancelot and Asquith stand at the edge of the ruined landscape. Asquith cannot look at his brother. Asquith has been wandering his drowned and ruined landscape all day. His clothes are torn and muddy.

Lancelot I am going to stay on a few days and try to calm Lord Heywood. He's threatening to bring in that bastard Chambers.

Asquith The opening of the sluice . . . I couldn't foresee –

Lancelot Grand idea. Let Chambers clean up this mess. I've got six commissions in front of me. I will let it be known, of course, that this was not your fault.

Asquith I . . . thank you.

Lancelot But it is your failure. (*short cough*) If you had not been distracted by the sensual heat of today . . . (*short cough*) If you had kept your mind on the future . . . and a wife.

Asquith I am. So . . . I am . . .

Lancelot Your fault, Asquith, is that you cannot honour the inherent tragedy of this work: that we will never see the glory of our landscapes. It takes fifty years for them to come into their own. And we'll be dust by then. But England still holds fast to a vision about herself. And

though in the prese
of this vision, in her
into an ever-growing
powerful tenderness. A
in that perfected 'morr
smell her own new mor
that she still dreams. (*Be*

The two brothers regar
Lancelot exits.

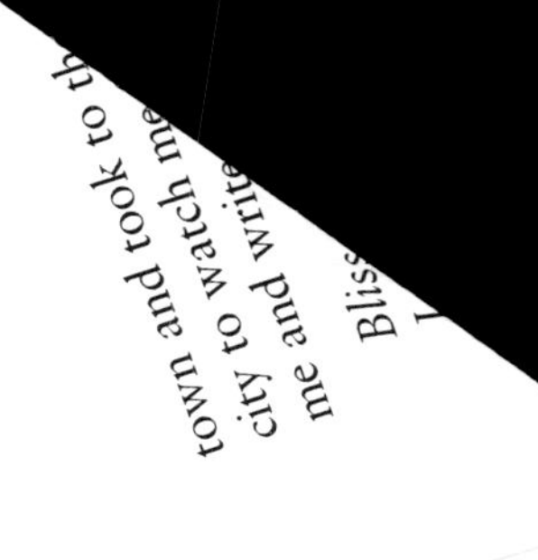

SCENE T – 1

Asquith walks the ruined landscape. He is exhausted. He picks up a handful of mud.

Asquith Who will wake me from this country? (*Beat.*) This. This was the church I raised from grass and dirt. Nothing now but drowned land. The sun rolls its wheel over my back and the villagers laugh. Months and months of work. Lord Heywood's servants whisper at my back. Mud beetle. Weed man. Crooked mile. The soldiers are going home. The river turns its back on me. The broken trees sleep without dreams. It is not right. This was my country. I tasted her. I tasted her and she tasted of oceans and spices and faraway worlds. And now? – (*He tastes the mud.*) I don't know. I don't know. A world. A world leaning into the future, a world that did not look back. That could have been our paradise. (*He looks over his shoulder as though he fears something.*)

Split scene: Jayfort appears elsewhere on stage, shadow-boxing. His professional moves are now a culmination of the various moves we saw earlier.

Jayfort First learned how to box in the fields, on the body of a friend. Then I went back down to London

e ring. Folk come from all over the
e fight. A man named Steward. Watches
s. Showed me his notebook once. He wrote:

appears in a patch of light, elsewhere on stage.
ayfort is not aware of her.

Bliss
For I am the last gleanings of the summer fruit –

Jayfort Not sure of the connection. Yet. I just box. (*Chants as he boxes.*)

Small girl's bones
At last they found
Seems she flew up
Right out of the ground.

Bliss (*chants*)
Bound, bound. Bound to this world.
Now bound for the deepest sea.

Jayfort
The killer that killed is killed you see
The murderer that murdered is he still free?
Venison, venison –

Bliss/Jayfort
Venison meat.
Run along, run along, run along feet.

Bliss disappears. Jayfort and Asquith are alone on stage.

Jayfort
I'm entertainment, dance, hit and chat
But I can read and write
Draw a map of the Caribbean.
Can you do that?
Rat, a tat, tat.

Asquith Listen. Shhh. The years are coming up from behind us, fast, fast, hear how they choke on their own thick breath?

Jayfort's shadow-boxing slows.

Jayfort Others are fiddlers, drummers, shipbuilders and dozens of languages I can hear but yet not understand and they all come to see me do the latest London dance. Sometimes there's blood but mostly –

Jayfort/Asquith – it's the roar in my head and the roar –

Jayfort – on the ground that keeps me up and going.

Asquith A world that could forget itself. A kind of happiness.

Jayfort It's sure not easy.

Asquith That would have been my England.

Jayfort But on a good night, a real good night in the ring, I can smell the ocean behind me, and my hands are swimming in the air, and the eyes in the back of my head are open wide as a continent, and –

Jayfort/Asquith – I don't rest –

Jayfort – and I'm never still –

Jayfort/Asquith – never still –

Jayfort stops boxing.

Jayfort – and this is my –

Asquith, on his knees, lowers his head, as if in prayer.

Jayfort/Asquith – peace.

Lights go out on Asquith. Jayfort is alone on stage.

Jayfort This is my. Paradise.

Jayfort swings hard twice, then blackout.

The following books are a selection of those used by the author for background research for her play

Bermingham, Ann. *Landscape and Ideology: the English Rustic Tradition, 1740–1860*. University of California Press, 1986.

Bolster, Jeffrey W. *Black Jacks: African-American Seamen in the Age of Sail*. Harvard University Press, 1997.

Gerzina, Gretchen. *Black England: Life before Emancipation*. London: John Murray, 1995.

Goldsmith, Oliver. *The Deserted Village*. London: Sampson Low, Marston, Low and Searle, 1875.

Hinde, Thomas. *Capability Brown: the Story of a Master Gardener*. London: Hutchinson, 1986.

Hoskins, W. G. *The Making of the English Landscape*. Penguin Books, 1985.

Hunt, John Dixon. *The Figure in the Landscape*. Johns Hopkins University Press, 1989.

Hyams, Edward. *Capability Brown and Humphrey Repton*. New York: Scribner's Sons, 1971.

Linebaugh, Peter. *The London Hanged: Crime and Civil Society in the Eighteenth Century*. Cambridge University Press, 1992.

McLeod, Bruce. *The Geography of Empire in English Literature, 1580–1745*. Cambridge University Press, 1999.

Stroud, Dorothy. *Capability Brown*. London: Faber and Faber, 1975.

Williams, Raymond. *The Country and the City*. New York: Oxford University Press, 1973.

Discover the brightest and best in fresh theatre writing with Faber's new StageScripts

Sweetheart by Nick Grosso (0571 17967 3)
Mules by Winsome Pinnock (0571 19022 7)
The Wolves by Michael Punter (0571 19302 1)
Gabriel by Moira Buffini (0571 19327 7)
Skeleton by Tanika Gupta (0571 19339 0)
The Cub by Stephanie McKnight (0571 19381 1)
Fair Game by Rebecca Prichard (0571 19476 1)
(a free adaptation of **Games in the Backyard** by Edna Mazya)
Crazyhorse by Parv Bancil (0571 19477 x)
Sabina! by Chris Dolan (0571 19590 3)
I Am Yours by Judith Thompson (0571 19612 8)
Been So Long by Che Walker (0571 19650 0)
Yard Gal by Rebecca Prichard (0571 19591 1)
Sea Urchins by Sharman Macdonald (0571 19695 0)
Twins by Maureen Lawrence (0571 20065 6)
Skinned by Abi Morgan (0571 20007 9)
Real Classy Affair by Nick Grosso (0571 19592 x)
Down Red Lane by Kate Dean (0571 20070 2)
Shang-a-Lang by Catherine Johnson (0571 20077 x)
The Storm by Alexander Ostrovsky
trs. Frank McGuinness (0571 20004 4)
By Many Wounds by Zinnie Harris (0571 20097 4)
So Special by Kevin Hood (0571 20044 3)
The Glory of Living by Rebecca Gilman (0571 20140 7)
Certain Young Men by Peter Gill (0571 20191 1)
Paddy Irishman, Paddy Englishman and Paddy . . . ?
by Declan Croghan (0571 20128 8)
Pelleas and Melisande by Maurice Maeterlinck
trs. Timberlake Wertenbaker (0571 20201 2)
Martha, Josie and the Chinese Elvis
by Charlotte Jones (0571 20237 3)
My Best Friend by Tamsin Oglesby (0571 20566 6)
Dogs Barking by Richard Zajdlic (0571 20006 0)
All That Trouble That We Had by Paul Lucas (0571 20267 5)
The Bedsit by Paul Sellar (0571 20364 7)
Drink, Dance, Laugh and Lie by Samuel Adamson (0571 20442 2)
The Map Maker's Sorrow by Chris Lee (0571 20365 5)
Silence by Moira Buffini (0571 20445 7)
Bitter with a Twist by Simon Treves (0571 20479 1)
My Dad's Corner Shop by Ray Grewal (0571 20534 8)
Jump Mr Malinoff, Jump by Toby Whithouse (0571 20584 4)
The Waiting Room by Tanika Gupta (0571 20514 3)
Still Time by Stephanie McKnight (0571 20782 0)
The Slight Witch by Paul Lucas (0571 20935 1)
Behind the Scenes at the Museum by Bryony Lavery (0571 20911 4)
A Wedding Story by Bryony Lavery (0571 20906 8)
Belonging by Kaite O'Reilly (0571 20902 5)